Contents

Part 1

Introduction

The historical background: the First World War

The obvious, immediate cause of the First World War was the assassination in Sarajevo on 28 June 1914 of Archduke Franz Ferdinand of Austria by a Serbian nationalist, Gavrilo Princip. Austria accused Serbia of complicity in the murder, and, under pressure from Germany, refused to accept Serbia's conciliatory reply to the accusations. Russia, acting out her traditional role as the defender of all Slavs, intervened on Serbia's behalf.

What happened next was both predictable and terrible. Austria declared war on Serbia on 28 July 1914, and on 1 August Germany declared war on Russia. France stood ready to honour her alliance with Russia, and so, on 3 August, Germany declared war on France and on the following day invaded Belgium, taking the easiest route for an attack on France. (This course of action makes it quite clear that the Serbian affair was simply an excuse for embarking on a war: the theatre of war shifted to Western Europe which remained the focus of the whole war.)   Great Britain had long been bound by a treaty (of 1839) to defend Belgium in case of an attack, and so on the same day, 4 August, she declared war on Germany. Now the battle lines were drawn up; on one side stood the Allies: Great Britain, France, Belgium, Russia, Serbia and Japan (which however took little active part in the war). Later they were joined by Italy, Romania, Greece and the United States. Facing the Allies were the Central Powers: Germany, Austria-Hungary, Turkey and, later, Bulgaria.

The point to remember here is that with the sole exception of Great Britain, all the big European nations already had large armies standing ready for war, because they all had a system of conscription (compulsory military training of all able-bodied men). Britain introduced conscription in 1916. Until then, therefore, the British forces consisted of professional soldiers and volunteers (a fact which goes some way to explain the ardently patriotic poems, idealising war, which were characteristic of the early years of the war).

The two sides were soon engaged in battles, the so-called 'Battles of the Frontiers', fought over Lorraine, the Ardennes, the Sambre and around Mons, as Germany advanced through Belgium into France. On 2 September 1914 the battle of the Marne took place. In this battle the German forces were driven back, and the German plan to crush France (the Schlieffen plan, named after Field Marshal Alfred von Schlieffen, an ardent advocate of the plan) was shown to be a failure.

Instead of swift victory, both sides settled down to trench warfare with its pattern of advances and retreats from fixed positions, all paid for by a relentlessly rising tally of casualties.

This was the first large-scale war to employ modern weapons, and yet it was largely fought by soldiers using rifles, bayonets and hand-grenades, in trenches, dugouts, in vast (and primitive) underground networks of passages. Throughout the autumn, winter and spring months of year after year of the war, the battlefront was a sea of mud, with duckboards laid down to help men floundering in the mire as they fought across 'no man's land' – in places no more than 200 yards wide and encircled by barbed wire – which separated the two sides.

Heavy bombardment using the huge new guns was tried, without much success, because the shells hit indiscriminately, and created large craters in an already impassable terrain. The result was deadlock – a tragically apposite word. The Germans tried to break it by using poison gas, and very nearly succeeded before the Allied forces were equipped with gas masks. (One curious result of this experiment was a silent agreement never to use poison gas again: with all its horrors the Second War War never stooped to this – on the battlefield, that is. The civilians in the death camps were quite another matter.)

The next breakthrough in modern warfare was the tank, invented by the British in 1916, though its potential was never fully exploited in this conflict.

The roll-call of battles on the Western Front has a resonance rarely encountered in the Second World War (except perhaps for Stalingrad and Monte Casino): the first battle of Ypres (October 1914), Vimy Ridge and the second battle of Ypres (1915), Verdun and the Somme (1916). In these last two battles some 650,000 Germans, 420,000 British and 195,000 French soldiers lost their lives (according to some sources; the casualty figures vary as if even the statisticians found themselves incapable of dealing efficiently with such horrifying numbers). Verdun and the Somme mark the turning point in men's perception of the war. They were followed in 1917 by the battle of Arras and the third battle of Ypres (also known as Passchendaele).

In April 1917 the United States, already angry about German submarine attacks on American merchant ships, declared war on Germany, after discovering that Germany was attempting to recruit Mexico for the Central Powers. Though the tide of war was clearly turning against Germany, at least on the Western Front, Germany still counter-attacked in the spring of 1918, using a five-pronged movement (along the Somme, Lys, Aisne, along Noyon – Montdidier and Champagne – Marne). The Allies responded by their final offensive which lasted from September to 11 November 1918. On that day the Germans signed the Armistice, admitting defeat.

We have been concentrating on the Western Front so far, partly because this was the theatre of war in which the British army played a very prominent part, and in which therefore most of the poets to be discussed in these Notes fought, and partly because this was the front on which ultimately the outcome of the war was decided.

On the Eastern Front Germany and Austria-Hungary faced Russia. In August 1914 the Russian army was decisively defeated by the Germans at Tannenberg in Eastern Prussia. In Galicia and Poland the Austrian army was less successful and was forced to retreat. There never was a fixed line of trenches here, as on the Western Front. Instead, the line of battle swayed to and fro, as the opposing armies advanced and retreated. With Germany playing a decisive part, however, the Central Powers were gradually driving the Russian army eastward.

Turkey, which joined the Central Powers in 1914, attacked Russia in the Caucasus. Great Britain and France tried to help Russia by landing troops on the Gallipoli peninsula in 1915, in an attempt to link up with the Russian forces, but the operation (in which Australian and New Zealand troops took part in large numbers) was a failure, and in early 1916 the Allied troops withdrew.

The huge losses suffered by the Russian army in vain, and the failure of their military apparatus, created a mood of anger and bitterness among the Russian people. On 12 March 1917 a revolution broke out and seven days later Czar Nicholas II resigned (as we now know, he and his family were shot in July 1918 at Ekaterinburg – later renamed Sverdlovsk). A provisional moderate government was set up under Alexander Kerensky.

With German assistance, however, Vladimir Ilyich Lenin, the exiled leader of the radical revolutionary party, returned to Russia and seized power. Thus the new Soviet Russia was born, and the Eastern Front ceased to exist. Preoccupied with their own civil wars, the Russians were ready to sign the peace of Brest-Litovsk with Germany in March 1918. The terms were harsh, though Germany was not to retain all her territorial gains from Russia when her own turn came to sue for peace in November 1918.

There was fighting on the Mediterranean Front too, where Allied armies defeated Bulgaria at Salonika in September 1918, and in Italy where Austria-Hungary suffered a crushing defeat.

The war spread to the Middle East as well where the British and Empire (now of course Commonwealth) troops defeated Turkey in Mesopotamia and in Palestine, effectively putting an end to Turkish rule there. On 30 October 1918 both Turkey and Austria-Hungary asked for a ceasefire.

It was inevitable that any war involving Britain should include naval warfare. While British merchant ships suffered heavy losses through the action of German U-boats (submarines), Britain fought and defeated the German Imperial Navy, with the decisive battle taking place in the North Sea off Jutland on 31 May 1916.

This was the first war in which aircraft were used, though mostly for reconnaissance and in support of land operations. The Germans used the Zeppelins (airships) to bomb British cities between 1915 and 1917, but the bombing of Britain was never on the scale of the bombing in the Second World War, and there were no retaliatory raids on German cities

Taken all in all, the First World War was really a European war, fought largely by European nations on European soil. The biggest battles, with the heaviest casualties, took place on the Western Front, in an area stretching from Flanders, in Belgium, across north-eastern France down to the Swiss border. It was this devastated land that took hold of men's imagination. It is impossible to glorify war against such a background, but we can and do acknowledge the extraordinary flowering of poetry born out of horror and rage, that took place there.

This summary opened by mentioning an obvious cause of the war, the assassination of Archduke Franz Ferdinand. Consider, however, the casualties of this war:

Allies:	Russia	1,700,000 men killed
	France	1,357,800
	British Empire	908,300
	Italy	650,000
	Romania	335,700
	United States	116,500
Central Powers:	Germany	1,773,700
	Austria-Hungary	1,200,000
	Turkey	325,000

Almost 8.5 million men were killed in all, a figure which does not include the vast numbers of soldiers wounded, blinded, crippled, mentally deranged and gassed.

Can we accept the murder of the heir to the Austrian throne by a fanatical patriot as an adequate explanation for such carnage? There were, of course, other underlying causes working towards the explosion of war.

First of all, Germany was, and had been since her victory over France in 1870, in an expansionist mood. Hers was a militaristic culture, and her ambitions could only be expressed in war. She wanted her 'place in the sun'; there was a feeling in Germany that other European nations, foremost among them Britain and France, had had more than their fair share of the good things – the wealth of their colonial possessions, the resulting advantages to their industry and trade. German industry had developed greatly, and wanted now new markets – and an easier access to the overseas markets than the North and Baltic Seas.

In addition, there had always been throughout German history the urge to expand eastward. This *Drang nach Osten*, the pressure to advance eastward, was not in order to create new markets but rather to occupy and Germanise new territories. So there was territorial hunger as well as colonial ambitions and the need to find markets for a growing industry.

And there was also, on Germany's part, a self-pitying, self-justifying aggressiveness. Having come to the table too late to get what she wanted by (relatively) peaceful means, Germany saw aggression as a morally justified way of redressing the balance. (Europe was to witness a resurgence of this mood, fed by the harsh terms of the Treaty of Versailles of June 1919. Hitler used it brilliantly to lead Germany into yet another world war some twenty years later.)

Germany was in an aggressive mood, then – and Austria-Hungary followed the German lead. But what of the other European nations? Mention was made above of the large armies of conscripted men, trained and equipped for war. The size of these armies is astonishing and significant: in 1914 Russia had an army of 12 million men, France of nearly 8.5 million, Germany 11 million, Austria-Hungary 7.75 million (with Great Britain by contrast commanding an army of some 950,000 men, including colonial troops).

With such huge armies at their disposal perhaps it seemed natural and inevitable – to the generals at least – to make use of them? There was fear of war which had found expression in the system of alliances – the partnership of Germany and Austria, the British pledge to Belgium, the Russo-French treaty – but ironically these alliances ensured that the war spread right across Europe.

It may be that the sheer size of the conflict created a disbelief in the fast-growing catastrophe. Both sides were confident that this new type of war using modern weapons would be over by Christmas 1914, and this belief certainly helped to create a mood of acceptance of what was expected to be a short decisive action only.

Another factor contributing to the fatal restiveness in Europe was the dissatisfaction of the smaller nations within the large European multi-national empires. The 1848 revolutions which sprang up all over Europe and which had nationalist as well as political aims, had been harshly suppressed and the Germanising and Russifying policies employed by the rulers fostered the resentment felt by the subjugated smaller nations. Inevitably they saw in war their chance of a drastic change in the status quo. (Their ambitions were satisfied – up to a point – at the peace conferences of 1919, with results which we are still witnessing today: the break-up of Russia, of Czechoslovakia, of Yugoslavia.)

A number of reasons have been put forward here for this catastrophic war. Ultimately, of course, none of them can offer a satisfactory explanation; the war can only be seen as an act of collective madness. It had been glorified as the Great War, the war to end all wars, but such fine phrases have gone out of fashion, perhaps because they fail to explain or justify a tragic folly of such magnitude.

England in 1914: the Edwardian summer

There have been many nostalgic accounts of England in the golden years of the Edwardian era. As in the land of Tennyson's Lotus-eaters, it seemed to be always afternoon there, the afternoon of a perfect summer day.

In truth, of course, it was a delightful period to live in if you happened to belong to the comfortable middle class, let alone to the upper classes. (The other side of the coin is shown very clearly in, for instance, the recollections of the maids and gardeners employed in large Suffolk country houses, which are to be found in Ronald Blythe's *Akenfield* – a very revealing book.)

It was a deeply class-ridden society, not the less so because the stratification was accepted and there was no very strong sense of social justice. Some steps had been taken to ameliorate the lot of the poor, notably the 1911 National Insurance Act, passed by Winston Churchill when he was Home Secretary. In the field of education nothing was done between the 1870 Elementary Education Act and the revolutionary 1944 Education Act (and it took another war to achieve this). There was no proper Health Service, no unemployment benefit, no really adequate old age pension; all this made employment desperately important, and the hunger for work created a buyer's market for the employers.

This was very much a 'Two Nations' Britain, and the working class was still largely of no account. We may wonder whether there was a causal link between this view of the lower half of a divided society, and the apparent readiness of the generals to sacrifice men in such vast numbers to ill-conceived military strategies.

But for those fortunate enough to belong to the privileged section of society, cheap domestic labour, low income tax, cheap imported food (from the colonies), all made for a very pleasant, civilised way of life. There was a sense of security, of an established, immovable order, of political stability, such as was never to be experienced again in Britain, or anywhere else.

It is interesting to note the extent to which the literature of this Edwardian and Georgian (so called after George V who succeeded to the throne in 1910) age reflects its tastes and values. The writers and their readership were largely in accord, accepting the same moral and aesthetic standards, apparently never questioning them.

It all sounds a little dull perhaps, and it may be that some of the initial patriotic enthusiasm with which the young volunteers greeted the war was due to an unacknowledged relief at a chance to escape the boredom of an over-secure existence.

Most of the poets of the First World War were born into this civilised, tolerant, unexceptionable section of society. A glance at the brief biographies in Part 2 of these Notes is sufficient. With a very few exceptions (such as Isaac Rosenberg and Wilfred Owen) they came mostly from the comfortable middle class or the aristocracy, and were public school boys and Oxbridge men. They were therefore perhaps the last generation to have a thorough grounding in the classics, and they went to the Front with their heads full of Hellenic ideals of heroism, of Hector, of the Spartans at Thermopylae. The majority of them volunteered out of hazy idealism, out of patriotism: perhaps to defend their country, perhaps to defend their ideal of honour. Their motives may seem unclear to us, and how could they be otherwise in a war fought for such confused, inadequate reasons?

They made their impression on the army, these idealistic young men. It was the first major war in British history in which gentlemen of breeding and education (the phrase may sound affected to us, but it had quite a precise meaning then) took an active part instead of leaving the fighting to professional soldiers. The newspapers of the time made much of the distinction between the idealistic volunteers and the professional army, the mercenaries (A. E. Housman's 'Epitaph on an Army of Mercenaries', written in 1914, restored to the latter their own dignity and worth as professionals doing their job).

In his *Undertones of War* (1928) Edmund Blunden tells us how pleased his Colonel was to discover that Lieutenant Blunden's volume of poetry had been favourably reviewed in *The Times Literary Supplement*. Many of these young volunteers wrote poetry, expressing their enthusiasm and their willingness to serve their country. It does not take much imagination to picture the impact of trench warfare on such idealism. Certainly there was heroism to be witnessed among both the officers and the ordinary soldiers, but it was inevitable that the heroic ideals would be shattered by the callousness with which the High Command could accept – and indeed demand – a constant stream of heavy casualties.

These were young men who had been sheltered from the harsher aspects of life by their background and upbringing, by their acceptance of their secure, privileged position. The society they belonged to was perhaps smug, but it had its decent values, its charitableness, its gentle virtues. From this, from the Oxbridge reading parties, from the village cricket matches, from tea on the vicarage lawn, they went into the blood-splattered mud of the trenches, and made their adjustments, drawing first on their pity for the men who were their responsibility, and then on their own bitter anger.

A note on the texts

The poems discussed in detail in Part 2, 'Summaries', can be found in the anthologies listed below; all are currently available. The alphabet letter preceding each title is also used on the Contents page and in the 'Summaries' section to indicate which anthologies contain which poems. It is also used in Part 3, 'Commentary', along with the title of any additional poem referred to but not dealt with in detail in Part 2, to enable the student to find a version of it.

(G) GARDNER, B. (ED.): *Up the Line to Death: The War Poets 1914–1918*, Methuen, London, 1964.

(M) MARTIN, CHRISTOPHER: *War Poems*, Collins Educational, London, 1991.

(C) PARSONS, I. M. (ED.): *Men who March Away: Poems of the First World War*, Chatto, London, 1965.

(R) REILLY, C. S. (ED.): *Scars Upon My Heart: Women's Poetry and Verse of the First World War*, Virago, London, 1981.

(P) SILKIN, JON (ED.): *The Penguin Book of First World War Poetry*, Penguin, Harmondsworth, 1971.

(O) STALLWORTHY, JON (ED.): *The Oxford Book of War Poetry*, Oxford University Press, Oxford, 1984.

Part 2

Summaries
of SELECTED POEMS

Note: The poems discussed in these Summaries have been chosen firstly, because they have unquestioned intrinsic literary merit or historical, documentary significance; secondly, because of the importance attached to them by various examining boards; and lastly and quite simply, because the author of these Notes likes them. The poems are arranged alphabetically by author.

Richard Aldington (1892–1962)

Educated at Dover College and London University. He served on the Western Front from 1916 to 1918, and was badly gassed. After the war he lived mostly in the South of France for the sake of his health, while pursuing a literary career. He published translations from the classics and from French literature, and wrote poetry. Aldington became the leading English poet of Imagism, a movement founded by Ezra Pound in the United States and T. E. Hulme in England, which strove rather self-consciously to employ 'images', precise representations of thought and emotion combined. He is best remembered for his bitter anti-war novel, *The Death of a Hero* (1929).

Battlefield (*C/O*)

This short poem presents a clear picture of a wintry battleground somewhere on the Western Front. It is a barren land, the houses destroyed, the ground torn by shells. The only things that grow there are the crosses marking the graves of the fallen soldiers.

  The diction and the images are spare, harsh, cold, but the conclusion of the second stanza presents an implied contrast to the icy chill. Here, in a part of France that had suffered so much through the war, close to the destroyed village, someone had felt pity for the dead German soldier, asking the passers-by (how many in that silent landscape?) to pray for him.

NOTES AND GLOSSARY:
shell-rent: torn by shells and grenades
fruitless land/Thorny with wire: in this barren land barbed wire seems to
                grow like a strange thorny plant

Ci-gît: (*French*) here lies; a phrase to be found only on tombstones

Ci-gît ... *pour lui*: (*French*) here lies a German soldier, pray for him. The repetition of the phrase stresses the vast numbers of the dead

Edmund Blunden (1896–1974)

Blunden spent his childhood at Yalding, Kent, where his father was a schoolmaster, and was educated at Christ's Hospital, Horsham, Sussex, and, after the war, at Queen's College, Oxford.

In 1916, when he should have gone up to Oxford, he enlisted instead, and went to France with the Royal Sussex Regiment. He survived the terrible battles of the Somme, Ypres and Passchendaele, winning the Military Cross. After the war he went up to Oxford but left without a degree. A gifted teacher, he taught English at the University of Tokyo in the twenties and again in the late forties, was Fellow and Tutor in English Literature at Merton College, Oxford, from 1931 to 1943. From 1953 to 1964 he was Professor of English Literature at the University of Hong Kong, and in 1964–8 Professor of Poetry at Oxford University.

All his life he was concerned with English literature, teaching and writing. His writing mirrors closely his two lifelong concerns: his love of the Southern English countryside, and his compulsion constantly to bear witness to the slaughter of the battles of the First World War, as if by doing so he could atone for having survived the war when so many others did not.

As well as in his poetry he recorded his war experiences in a prose memoir, *Undertones of War* (1928), which also includes thirty-two of his war poems. *Undertones of War* ranks with Robert Graves's *Goodbye to All That* (1929) and Siegfried Sassoon's *Memoirs of an Infantry Officer* (1930) as the best prose to come out of the war. (Blunden knew both these men well, and Sassoon especially was a close friend.) In this prose memoir, as in his poetry, we are constantly made aware how desperately Blunden clung to his memories of the English countryside and to his belief that all-healing nature will in the end conquer war and that even the blighted war landscape will come to life again.

He was much liked in his regiment, was nicknamed 'Bunny' or 'Rabbit' for his youthful shyness, and was treated with fatherly kindness. Yet there was a dark, tough side to his nature. He won the Military Cross for bravery in action, and right through the war he carried in his pocket Edward Young's death-obsessed poetical meditations, *Night Thoughts*.

He lies buried in the grassy churchyard at Long Melford, Suffolk, a fitting resting-place for this 'harmless young shepherd in a soldier's coat', as he called himself.

The Zonnebeke Road (C/P/O)

The soldiers are returning from night watch duty, frozen to the marrow. It is a dull winter morning, with heavy skies above the desolate blasted landscape, which matches the men's mood of defiant despair. They have no hope of victory, of returning home, yet they will not flinch. Hoping for nothing, contemptuous of death, they can be ready to face whatever the future brings.

There is a dissonance, perhaps deliberate, between the jingling regular rhymes, some of them rather forced ('perhaps' . . . 'some corpse's chaps'), and the grim subject matter.

NOTES AND GLOSSARY:

this late withered light: the sun rose late and is shining feebly

wont: accustomed to (Blunden still uses from time to time the old-fashioned 'poetic' diction, which was to disappear from war poetry altogether)

stand down: go off duty

the bended bone: the very bones of the soldiers' hands are frozen in position, clasping the rifles

dugout: space dug out in the trenches to provide shelter from enemy fire for the soldiers

seeming-saturnine: wearing a gloomy appearance

Haymarket: the soldiers named parts of the trenches after parts of London or other places in Britain

minenwerfers: (*German*) mine-throwers

have it to the inch: know it to the last detail (and can aim their mines accurately)

Piteous and silly: the driven snow looks out of place, unfitting for this grim landscape in its delicacy

fang the plain: a startlingly effective image: the tree stumps like broken teeth surround the plain. The image extends from the sky pressing down like a swollen cheek to the distorted 'gargoyle' shriek from a frozen throat

bine: stem of a climbing plant

oozes into dun: creeps slowly into the dirty fog

Ypres: altogether there were three battles of Ypres (see the Introduction above, p. 8), as well as continuous outbreaks of fighting in between

fond fool: silly fool

tour: period of duty

screaming dumbness: this bringing together of two contradictory terms is an often used and very effective poetic device, called the oxymoron

that one hope, disdain: all the men can offer in response to the horror round them is their proud defiance, hoping for nothing

---

Vlamertinghe: Passing the Château, July 1917 (*C/P/O*)

The soldiers are marching past the Vlamertinghe château gardens on their way into battle, and the poet asks ironically whether they should be garlanded with flowers like the beasts led to be sacrificed at pagan altars. He lists the flowers and their splendid colours, but his admiration is again tinged with irony; the bright red of the poppies should be much duller – like dried blood. (We may remember here the deep significance of the Flanders poppies: the soldiers did believe that these flowers owed their brilliant red colour to all the blood spilled into the ground in which they grew. A poem by a Canadian doctor, John McCrae (1872–1918), published in 1915 under the title of 'In Flanders Fields' summed up the almost mystical significance of these poppies, and became immensely popular. The symbolism of the poppy was the reason for the paper poppies sold on street corners to commemorate Armistice Day, a custom still observed today.)

NOTES AND GLOSSARY:

'And all her silken flanks ... drest': the poem opens with a quotation from John Keats's 'Ode on a Grecian Urn' describing a scene depicted on a Grecian vase, in which a priest is leading a heifer to be sacrificed at the altar. The ironical comparison between the beast and the soldiers, all led to slaughter, can hardly be missed. We might recall here Owen's line in 'Anthem for Doomed Youth': 'What passing-bells for these who die as cattle?'

not yet gone West: not yet been killed: should the soldiers who are still alive be garlanded with flowers like the sacrificial beast? The poem was inspired by the incongruous sight of the château garden full of flowers even so near the battlefield. Perhaps some of the soldiers in a mood of defiant gaiety had picked flowers for button-holes

borrows grace for grace: wears a graceful appearance to maintain its dignity

Spite of: in spite of

brute guns lowing: notice the use of the verb 'lowing': the guns bellow like cattle, reminding us again of the sacrificial heifer in Keats's poem

La Quinque Rue (P)

This is the description of a nightmare. The soldier walking along a quiet road at night sees it turning into the old battleground. The images are full of horror: even the hedges have talons like birds of prey. (We might recall here that Siegfried Sassoon imagined that he saw corpses strewn along Piccadilly.)

The quiet apologetic ending is all the more effective after the dreadful vision of the road.

NOTES AND GLOSSARY:

forlorn effigies of farms: the pitiful ruins of farmhouses
lustrous mercy: kindly moonlight
foul-gorged: fed greedily on rotten flesh
dreadful rags/Fur ... banks: these few words sum up the horror: the roadside is thickly covered with ragged corpses hanging on barbed wire
Why clink those spades: perhaps to dig trenches, perhaps to dig graves
wet and crawling: the grass is wet with blood, full of crawling maggots
countersign: password which must be given to the sentry to show that the new arrivals are friends, not enemies. The countersign was changed daily
turning blood to glass: freezing the blood with horror

1916 seen from 1921 (C/P)

This poem encapsulates what was to remain an abiding theme with Blunden: his memories of the war remained so strong that they blocked out the present. The peaceful English landscape is overlaid with the images and sounds of the battlefield. His recollection of a small chapel to which he and his best friend used to go in order to escape from the war is still brilliantly vivid ('bright as blood' is his telling phrase): he cannot forget.

NOTES AND GLOSSARY:

the grey rags: the torn uniforms of dead German soldiers hanging on the barbed wire
drags/Its wounded length: the image is that of a wounded animal
the charred stub ... tree: the poet sees more clearly the burnt-down tree stump on the battlefield of his memory than the growing English tree in front of him
none's at home in vain: nobody is waiting at home for someone who will never return
redoubt: enclosed deep trench, protected on all sides

the grudging wars: the war was unwilling to let them have even a brief
moment of peace
Shrewd: sharply, bitingly

Rupert Brooke (1887–1915)

Born and educated at Rugby School where his father was a master, Brooke
won a classics scholarship to King's College, Cambridge. He had a
brilliant undergraduate career, was a founder member of the Marlowe
Dramatic Society, joined the Fabian Society (thus hinting at the possible
transformation – if he had lived – of one 'Magnificently unprepared/For
the littleness of life' as Frances Cornford described him). To add to his
reputation he was invited to join the Apostles, the élite undergraduate
debating society. Surprisingly, his undergraduate career closed with a
Second in his English Tripos in 1909.

After travel on the Continent he began work on his dissertation on the
Jacobean dramatist John Webster, as well as writing poetry. His *Poems*
came out in 1911, and his verse (including the delightful 'The Old
Vicarage, Grantchester' and 'The Fish') appeared in *Georgian Poetry*,
1911–12 Series, edited by Sir Edward Marsh (1872–1953). Marsh became
a close friend, fell deeply in love with Brooke and it was said that he never
recovered from Brooke's death.

In spring 1913 Brooke was awarded his Fellowship at King's and
seemed on course for a distinguished academic career, but he had been
through an unhappy love affair which affected him deeply. So, before
taking up his Fellowship, he embarked on world-wide travels.

He returned to England in June 1914, and when the war broke out, he
enlisted at once, and was offered a commission in the Royal Naval Divi-
sion. He saw action at Antwerp in 1914 (a fact often overlooked in the
comments on this poet of warlike enthusiasm who died *en route* to war).
His ship was sent to Gallipoli in early 1915, and Brooke died of blood
poisoning caused by a mosquito bite on the island of Skyros on 17 April
1915, and was buried there. There is a curious parallel between his manner
of dying and that of another romantic figure of English literature, Lord
Byron, who died of marsh fever at Missolonghi in Greece, while preparing
to join the Greek fight for liberty.

Brooke's literary reputation grew out of his legendary undergraduate
years, and was confirmed by the five '1914' sonnets, written on his
Christmas leave in 1914 and published in *1914 and Other Poems* in 1915.
The adulation these poems received had much to do with the patriotic
mood of the country. Vera Brittain in her *Testament of Youth* (1933)
describes them as 'unhackneyed, courageous and almost shattering in their
passionate, relevant idealism', and her words are a salutary reminder of
how people regarded the war at first.

Most critics now believe that had he lived, Brooke would have changed not only his themes, but his style as well, discarding the grandiloquent, self-regarding rhetoric. Charles Hamilton Sorley, who was killed later in the same year, pinpointed the basic fault in the '1914' sonnets. In a letter to his mother he said that Brooke was 'far too obsessed with his own sacrifice, regarding the going to war of himself (and others) as a highly intense, remarkable and sacrificial exploit' – in other words that it was, in Brooke's view, his own great worth that made his sacrifice great.

But forget for the present Brooke as a legend, and read the poems for themselves. You may find them much more rewarding than you had expected.

Peace (G/M/C/O)

There is a stridency in the rhetoric of this poem which alienates; yet the poem repays study. It illuminates a state of mind that made the war an attractive proposition. Undoubtedly there were many other young men who felt like Brooke that their world was tired and their lives stagnant, and who, like he, hoped to find a new purpose in the war of their imagination. They spoke of patriotism, of fighting for their country, but no doubt much of their enthusiasm stemmed from their delight in finding a purpose, a challenge. In this way 'Peace' is a footnote to the statistics of thousands of volunteers enlisting.

NOTES AND GLOSSARY:

Peace: is there irony between the title and the subject of the poem? If so, it is unintentional: Brooke did find peace in his brief war experiences after the private turmoils of the preceding years

matched us ... hour: made us capable of measuring up to the demands of a just war. The crusading note rings false in the light of later events. Brooke's vision of the war has nothing in common with the reality of the muddy trenches, and, as in most of the poetry of the early years of the war, we find here a complete acceptance of the war as just and necessary. We may note in passing that religious undertones, such as we find here, are noticeably absent in the majority of the war poems. The self-disgust and the hope of finding a satisfying purpose in the war are sincere

all the little emptiness of love: presumably Brooke is thinking of his unhappy love affair

that has ending: that will stop

the worst friend ... is but Death: once we have conquered our fear of death we have nothing to fear. There is an echo here of the Bible, I Corinthians 15:26, 'The last enemy that shall be destroyed is death'

The Dead (C/P)

While the first stanza is a catalogue of the pleasures of living, the second stanza is an extended metaphor of death. Like frost freezing the dancing water to ice, death freezes the movement of life, leaving a miraculous peace and silence ('A width, a shining peace'). There is a feeling of detachment here, that embraces death without emotion: it is a far cry from poetry like Owen's and Sassoon's, racked by pity and terror.

NOTES AND GLOSSARY:
Washed ... with sorrow: purified by unhappiness
Swift to mirth: laughing easily
a gathered radiance: a concentrated brilliant light

The Soldier (P/O)

This is the most famous of Rupert Brooke's five sonnets, undoubtedly to some extent at least because here Brooke was unwittingly writing his own epitaph. What moves the reader also is the sense of Brooke's genuine deep love of England and its people. This is no empty rhetoric: the opening line speaks of death simply and modestly. The poet wishes to be remembered as part of England, of her gentle ways and quiet people.

You might like to compare Brooke's sonnet to Thomas Hardy's 'Drummer Hodge', written earlier, during the Boer war. There are similarities between the two poems, and there are significant differences: Hardy comes closer to the realities of war (Drummer Hodge is thrown into his grave, without a coffin, without any funeral rites).

NOTES AND GLOSSARY:
a richer dust: is there a hint here of Brooke's high valuation of his sacrifice?
A pulse in the eternal mind: at one with God, a part of His divinity
Gives somewhere back ... given: the ways of thinking which he had learnt in England will be transmuted back to England somehow, perhaps through his poetry. Throughout the poem there rings a note of gratitude for what his country had given him, as well as an unquestionable awareness of his own high worth (as C. H. Sorley had pointed out)

May Wedderburn Cannan (1893–1973)

A poet and novelist, she was born in Oxford and educated at Wychwood School. During the War she served with the Voluntary Aid Detachment as a nurse (a V.A.D.), and also worked for the Intelligence Service. She was engaged to Sir Arthur Quiller-Couch's son Bevil, who died of influenza during the terrible epidemic of 1918 which killed so many soldiers and civilians. After his death she worked for Oxford University Press in Oxford for a number of years, and later was assistant librarian at the Athenaeum Club in London. She married Brigadier P. J. Slater.

Rouen, 26 April–25 May 1915 (*R/O*)

The poet remembers her days as a V.A.D. at Rouen, the port 50 kilometres up the River Seine where newly arrived soldiers from England disembarked, and where the Red Cross barges collected the wounded on their way to hospital ships and to England. The first eight stanzas alternate descriptions of Rouen at different times of day with questions urging the poet to remember those days. After that there are just the urgent questions, pressing her to remember.

Rouen and her place in it are described in a series of images, often consisting just of a word or two, and the mostly fifteen-syllable anapaestic lines (two unstressed syllables followed by a stressed one) emphasise the haste to describe, to leave nothing out. The poem does not need the phrase 'Eastwards to the sea' to recall Rudyard Kipling's poems with their lists (though he is of course a far more accomplished versifier).

It succeeds in conveying the young nurse's delight in her work, her pride in helping the wounded and cheering up the soldiers on their way to the Front. We must remember, of course, that this poem was written during the early part of the war, before the slaughter began in earnest with the great battles of 1916.

NOTES AND GLOSSARY:
tatties: screens or mats
Woodbines: cheap cigarettes sold to the soldiers in the canteen
Drafts: soldiers newly arrived from England
stood to save the King: stood at attention for the national anthem
firing blue the window-pane: daylight suddenly turning the darkness outside to blue

Elizabeth Daryush (1887–1976)

Born in London, daughter of the Poet Laureate, Robert Bridges, she was educated at home by private tutors, as befitted her privileged background. She published three volumes of poetry in 1911, 1916 and 1921, but in later years dismissed them as of no importance. As a poet's daughter she took a good deal of interest in the technique of verse writing, though in her own poems she employed conventional metres and rhyme schemes. In 1923 she married Ali Akbar Daryush, and for a number of years lived with her husband in his native Persia (Iran).

Subalterns (R/O)

This short poem captures neatly the gap between the gushing young ladies at home and the officers back from the war. It is a sardonic comment on mutual incomprehension. On the one side, the admiring girl who pictures the war as glorious, and the coming of peace as an unadulterated joy; on the other, the returning young officer, struggling inarticulately to explain his contradictory emotions. He cannot forget the horrors of the war, yet at the same time he is aware of the war as a time of being intensely alive while under the threat of death. Inevitably his post-war existence seems dull by comparison. Notice the deliberate contrast between the young lady's high-flown clichés and the subaltern's slangy everyday language.

NOTES AND GLOSSARY:
The sunny hours they bought: the peace won at a high price
subalterns: junior officers, lowest in the army officer hierarchy

Robert Graves (1895–1985)

Born in London, the son of A. P. Graves, a poet and journalist of Irish descent. On his mother's side Graves was descended from the distinguished German historian Leopold von Ranke (Graves's middle name was von Ranke, a fact which made some of his fellow officers a bit suspicious of him at first).

He was educated at Charterhouse School which he loathed, and won a classical scholarship to St John's College, Oxford, but the outbreak of the war stopped him from taking it up.

When war was declared, he was at Harlech in North Wales, where the family had a holiday house. So it happened that he took a commission in the Royal Welch Fusiliers. He developed a great respect for his regiment and for the Welshmen he commanded.

He was sent to France quite quickly and plunged straight into trench warfare. He went through a good deal of heavy fighting and saw many of his friends killed. On 24 July 1916, his twenty-first birthday, he was shot through the head and lung, and in the confusion of the battle was reported dead of wounds, and his parents were informed accordingly. He survived, however, and spent his convalescence at Harlech with Siegfried Sassoon, whom he had met in France. The two men were to remain friends for many years.

In November 1916 he returned to France, but his damaged lung rendered him unfit for active service and he was sent back to England to convalesce at Somerville College, Oxford. In 1918 he married Nancy, daughter of the painter William Nicholson, by all accounts an unusual girl, an independent-minded feminist.

Graves was demobilised and in October 1919 he went up to Oxford at last, having already begun to make a name for himself as a poet (he had published two volumes of poetry during his time in the army, *Over the Brazier* (1916) and *Fairies and Fusiliers* (1917)). He found that he was too old and had been through too much to settle down to an undergraduate existence. He left Oxford without taking a degree, though he was awarded a B. Litt. by thesis in 1926. In the same year, having tried unsuccessfully to run a small shop in Oxford, he was offered the post of Professor of English Literature at the University of Cairo. The Graves family remained in Cairo until 1929. During this time he completed his autobiography, *Goodbye to All That*, judged by many to be the best account of the war.

In 1929 he and his wife parted company, after he became involved with the eccentric American poet Laura Riding. This stormy relationship lasted for some fourteen years, but broke up in the end. Graves had been living in Majorca with Laura, and he remained there more or less until his death, having got married again (to Beryl Pritchard). He went on writing poetry, historical novels (one of which, *I, Claudius*, was later turned into a very successful television series), and works on religious, mythological and anthropological subjects. From 1961 to 1966 he was Professor of Poetry at Oxford.

It should be noted that he excluded almost all his war poems from the later editions of his poetry.

A Dead Boche (*M*)

In this short poem Graves sets out to shock his readers, to shake them into a full realisation of the horrors of war. Brutal, unsparing in the description of the dead German – decomposing, stinking, his blood congealed to black – the poem is a powerful denunciation of the war which is all the more remarkable for having been written quite early in the war. In his *Goodbye to All That* Graves is restrained, holding himself back when describing death and madness all round him, but in this poem he speaks out, silencing all those who glorify war.

NOTES AND GLOSSARY:

Boche: a contemptuous French term for a German, taken over by British soldiers as well

Mametz Wood:	one of the many woods fought over on the Western Front
things unclean:	the description is deliberately left vague, forcing the readers to use their imagination in picturing the horror
crop-haired:	German soldiers wore their hair cut very short

Two Fusiliers (*G/C*)

The end of the war has come at last, and two friends from the Fusiliers battalion congratulate themselves on having survived. Their friendship has been cemented not by oaths and pledges, but by their common experiences in the war. They both expected to be killed, and having survived they find themselves ennobled by their brush with death. Through witnessing other men's death they felt more fully alive ('found ... In dead men breath').

It had been suggested that the two Fusiliers are Graves himself and Sassoon (who was also in the Royal Welch Fusiliers, though not in Graves's battalion). If that is so, there is sad irony in the proud boast of friendship in the poem; Sassoon took exception to some of Graves's remarks in *Goodbye to All That* (particularly about Wilfred Owen), and though in later editions Graves excised the offending passages, the friendship of the two poets never recovered.

NOTES AND GLOSSARY:

Close bound enough: bound sufficiently tightly

By wire and wood and stake: the two soldiers are bound together by their shared experiences of the trenches which were shored up with planks of wood, encircled by barbed wire fixed to wooden posts

Fricourt, Festubert: places fought over in Flanders, on the Western Front

By Picard clay: by their memories of the mud in the trenches in Picardy in eastern France, and also of the men buried there

Beauty in Death: having faced death and survived, the two men found a nobility of sorts in their experiences

In dead men breath: other men's death made them fully aware of being alive; the death of others had perhaps saved their own lives

Recalling War (*C/P/O*)

The poet looks back at the war with a sardonic eye. His wounds have healed (you will remember that Graves had been shot clean through the lung) and ache only when the weather is changing. Other men maimed by the war are also used now to their ghastly handicaps.

Graves recalls the madness of war, the hysterical mood of patriotic defiance. Death governed all their thoughts then, and, aware of his presence, the young men embraced the delights of a thoughtless hedonism, taking their pleasures, swearing and posturing.

All the old certainties of faith, of moral values were gone, all was madness under orders. Like children at play the soldiers knocked down buildings, their guns cut down whole forests like a child scything off dandelion heads with a stick. Seen from a distance the falling men looked like toy soldiers, the battles seemed just children's games. This is something to remember in the future, when the survivors have grown old, and are building up new visions founded on the despair of their souls.

The tone is flippant, the bitterness concealed under a pretence of acceptance. There is no rage in this controlled remembrance of the horrors. Sassoon once said that Graves seemed to be standing at attention when reading his poems aloud, and perhaps this habit of self-command dictates the form of this poem.

NOTES AND GLOSSARY:

silvered: covered with a shiny new skin
the nature-look of time: a seasoned natural appearance
discord of flags: quarrel between nations
infection of the common sky: the war hysteria that settled over Europe
Death was young again: Death was fashionable, vibrantly new
fate-spasm: death throes, the moment of death
God – /A word of rage: blasphemy was useful for venting one's anger
earth to ugly earth: an echo of the burial service of the Church of England ('earth to earth, ashes to ashes, dust to dust'), but given a new meaning by the ugly mud of the trenches
foundering of sublimities: the collapse of the old beliefs in the goodness of man, in virtue

Julian Grenfell (1888–1915)

Alone among the war poets, Grenfell was a professional soldier. The eldest son of Lord Desborough, educated at Eton and Balliol College, Oxford, he joined the army in 1910 as a regular officer. He saw service in India and South Africa with the Royal Dragoons. He went to France with his regiment, and was awarded a D.S.O. and was twice mentioned in dispatches. In April 1915 he died of wounds (his younger brother Billy, also a poet and due to be elected Fellow of All Souls, was killed two months later, the Bessborough title thus becoming extinct). Julian Grenfell wrote several poems in the army, but he is remembered for one poem alone, 'Into Battle', one of the most anthologised poems of the First World War.

Into Battle (*M/C/P/O*)

A striking feature of the poem is its neutrality. It is not about fighting *Germans*, it is about fighting as such, a noble, almost mystical heroic sacrifice, performed joyfully. The background is not the barbed wire and mud of Flanders, but a green, essentially English landscape in the spring, and the soldier is joined in fellowship by the trees, the woodland birds who will take him among themselves when he is dead. The great constellations in the sky will welcome him, as they welcomed the dead heroes of Greek legends.

Though he does describe the coming battle as 'the brazen frenzy', he hardly speaks of it. While waiting for the battle to begin, he learns from the horses their noble patience and their courage, and when the fighting begins he is possessed by 'the joy of battle', and though death is all round him, he is secure in his knowledge that nature – Day and Night – will take him as its own.

The poem is an oddity: though received with enthusiasm, it really has no place among the patriotic outpourings of the time, and once the full horrors of trench fighting became known Grenfell's poem seemed almost an embarrassment. Yet it cannot be mocked: it is too well written and deeply felt for that, and should perhaps be seen as a curious fruit of classical education. The Greeks lived in such a world of fellowship between man and nature, and they surely would have recognised the poet's 'joy of battle' better than any of the men who lived through the First World War.

NOTES AND GLOSSARY:

has increase: gains (the phrase has a biblical ring; see I Corinthians 3:6, 'God gave the increase')

The Dog-Star: Sirius, the brightest of all stars

the Sisters Seven: the Pleiades, a brilliant group of stars

Orion's Belt: Orion is a constellation of seven bright stars, three of which form Orion's sword-belt. These are all stars known to the ancients, and with their places firmly established in men's minds over the centuries

If this be the last song: it was Grenfell's last song, and he sang it well

joy of battle: an emotion known to the heroes of the ancient Greeks, and to the Norsemen (who had a name for it – *berserk*). Grenfell seems to be the only one to have experienced this and written of it. But could he have retained this high ideal of war after, say, the battle of the Somme, had he lived to take part in it?

Ivor Gurney (1890–1937)

Gloucestershire-born and bred, the son of a tailor, he was educated as a chorister at the High School, Gloucester, and his remarkable musical gifts won him an Open Scholarship to the Royal College of Music in London. From early on he wrote poetry as well as composing music, especially songs.

At the outbreak of the war he tried to join the Gloucestershire Regiment, but was turned down because of his weak eyesight. He finally succeeded in being accepted for active service in 1915, and went over to France in May 1916. In 1917 he took part in the Somme offensive, was wounded, recovered and was gassed and invalided out. In the same year he published a collection of poems, entitled *Severn and Somme*, and composed a good deal of music as well, but by 1918 it became clear that his war experiences had affected his already fragile mental state. In 1922 he was committed to an asylum in Gloucester. The rest of his life was spent in mental hospitals, some of it in the anguished belief that the war was still going on. At some time in the last years of his life he wrote a letter to the London Metropolitan Police which ends, heartrendingly: 'Asking for Death, Release or Imprisonment. And end to pain.'

The Silent One (*C/P/O*)

The poem contrasts two soldiers: one the cheerful NCO, chattering with a Buckinghamshire accent, who goes obediently forward to certain death at his officer's suggestion; the other, Gurney himself, sees clearly that to obey the officer's polite suggestion is to get killed, and so, with equal politeness, he declines to follow the first man, lies flat on the ground, thinks of music and waits for the crisis to pass.

NOTES AND GLOSSARY:

on the wires: on the barbed wire
unbroken wires: barbed wire with no opening through which a man might crawl forward
faithful to his stripes: doing his duty as a non-commissioned officer
and ended: and died
line: line of battle; organised formation to meet the enemy
finicking: finicky, exaggeratedly correct
Darkness, shot at: summing up of the poet's thoughts in verse
thought of music: thinking of music was to Gurney an escape, a way of dealing with the crisis in which he found himself

To His Love (*C/P/O*)

The poem starts quietly: it is no good making plans for walks in the Cotswolds because his friend is dead. The poet remembers him as athletic and quick-moving, rowing skilfully on the Severn. You could not recognise him now in the piece of bleeding flesh. He died bravely and it is right that he should be covered with flowers – but do it quickly to cover the ghastly sight that the poet must try to forget. (You might like to compare Gurney's poem, rooted in personal experience, with Charlotte Mew's 'The Cenotaph'. In the latter poem the mourning note is sincere but there is no such raw emotion as in Gurney, in what is necessarily a second-hand experience for Mew.)

In the first three stanzas there are references to Gurney's beloved Gloucestershire (the sheep on Cotswold hills, cropping the grass while the two friends walk by; rowing a boat on the Severn; violets picked on the Severn's banks). All control gives way in the last stanza which tries to blot out the unbearable sight. Gurney's love of the English countryside and his love for his dead friend are the two themes here, and they are two of the recurring themes of the poetry of the First World War (see Part 3, 'Commentary', pp. 61–6, 70–2).

NOTES AND GLOSSARY:

Under the blue: under the blue sky

You would not know him now: the dead man is hideously mangled

But still he died/Nobly: surely there is a quiet note of irony here: there can be no comfort in thinking of a hero's death when the man died so horribly

cover him soon!: there is real pain in the anguished exclamation. The writer cannot bear the dreadful sight

memoried: remembered from the past

that red wet/Thing: it is no longer recognisably a human body, just a mass of bloody flesh

Strange Hells (*P*)

This strange poem written after the war gives some indication of Gurney's mental state. He reveals the torment that the roar of the guns inflicted on him (perhaps as a musician he was particularly sensitive to noise). He remembers how during their first terrifying experience of heavy bombardment the Gloucesters managed to block out the roar and keep their sanity by singing over and over again the same catchy tune.

Abruptly the poem switches to the post-war present: the soldiers are now unemployed, or working as shop assistants, or, dressed in borrowed clothes, walking from town to town in search of work. They all must learn not to betray the inner hell of their memories: Gurney was clearly aware of his precarious mental balance, and of the need to camouflage his anguish. It is not a great poem, but it has the power to move the reader by offering glimpses of a mind cracking under the stress of war memories.

NOTES AND GLOSSARY:

put out: blotted out
with diaphragms fixed: with their chests tightened by terror
Après la guerre fini: when the war is over (a soldiers' song in soldiers' French)
eighteen pounders: guns firing shells weighing eighteen pounds
on State-doles: on unemployment benefit
tatterns: tatters (adapted to rhyme with patterns)

Thomas Hardy (1840–1928)

Born at Bockhampton, Dorset, the son of a stonemason, Hardy started life as an architect, being engaged mostly in church restoration work. He soon turned to literature, and wrote novels and short stories and, in his later years, poetry of a very high order. He became the foremost literary figure of his day, creating his own England, the fictional Wessex, as a background to his fiction. Though his plots are melodramatic at times, his powerful vision of the landscape of his imagination, and of men ruled by a relentless, unfeeling destiny, works a lasting spell on his readers. He seems to belong to the great nineteenth-century classics, and it may come as a surprise to find him included in these Notes, but he has earned a place among the poets of the First World War nevertheless. His 'Channel Firing', written in April 1914, is a strange prophetic vision of the war to come. While 'Men Who March Away (Song of the Soldiers; September 5, 1914)' captures the patriotic mood of the time, his masterly 'In Time of "The Breaking of Nations"', written a year later, directs our eyes beyond the war to peace and forgetting.

Already an old man when the war broke out, Hardy was nevertheless deeply affected by it and shaken out of his agnosticism. The few poems he wrote during the war speak with deep feeling and far-seeing authority.

Drummer Hodge (*M/P/O*)

Written *c.* 1899 during the Boer War (Britain's last imperialist war), the poem has no overt moral or pacific message. Yet it conveys quite clearly the belief that this young soldier died in a war he did not understand, in a country he knew nothing about, and that his life was thrown away just as heedlessly as his dead body was flung into its unconsecrated grave.

The stars that come out above his grave at night are not the constellations of home, for he lies in an alien land, in the Southern hemisphere. His ignorance is stressed, not to denigrate him, but to emphasise the injustice of his death for no cause that he could understand.

The poem certainly invites comparison with Rupert Brooke's 'The Soldier', especially in the last stanza. Where Brooke proudly appropriates a patch of foreign soil as 'forever England', because *he* lies buried there, poor Hodge lies forgotten in an unmarked grave, his decomposed body becoming part of the African soil, with the incomprehensibly alien stars looking down on him. Written in the first year of an earlier war, Hardy's poem prepares the way for the anti-war sentiments of the poets of the First World War.

NOTES AND GLOSSARY:

Hodge:	the name was probably chosen deliberately: 'Hodge' is a common nickname for the typical English countryman
kopje-crest:	top of a low hill (a *kopje* in Afrikaans)
veldt:	(*Afrikaans*) open grass-country in South Africa
Wessex:	Hardy's name for the south-western counties of England (Hampshire, Dorset, Wiltshire, parts of Berkshire and stretching west as far as Somerset), centring round Dorset, which are the setting of his Wessex novels. Wessex was originally a West Saxon kingdom which flourished in the sixth century
Karoo:	South African treeless plateau on which only scrub grows
The Bush:	wild uncultivated country
strange-eyed:	consisting of unfamiliar stars

A Wife in London (December 1899) (*M/P/O*)

The poem was written during the Boer War (1899–1902), but the sentiment it expresses holds true for any war. A soldier's wife is sitting alone on a foggy day in London when a messenger brings her the War Office telegram informing her of her husband's death in battle in the war in South Africa. The following day, which is even foggier and gloomier, a letter arrives from her dead husband, assuring her that he hopes to be back soon and telling her of his plans for their pleasure trips in the coming summer. It is a sad little tale, no doubt quite common in time of war, and it is told in an unemotional style, without a single comment that would betray the poet's own thoughts and feelings on the matter. No comment is made about the cruel late arrival of the letter, surely one of Hardy's 'Life's Little Ironies'. The single dramatic phrase 'whom the worm now knows' is of course all the more effective against the tone of the rest of the poem.

NOTES AND GLOSSARY:

tawny vapour: thick yellow London fog
webby: like a spider's web
whom the worm now knows: who is now dead and buried
in highest feather: in a very cheerful, optimistic mood
brake and burn: bracken and stream

Men Who March Away (Song of the Soldiers; September 5, 1914) (G/C/O)

This poem, written in September 1914, begins by questioning the men's decision to join in the war. The questions put in the first two stanzas are answered in the following three and the poem ends with a rewording of the opening questions which makes a resounding statement of the will to fight. The questions and answers are addressed to a doubtful bystander, the 'Friend with the musing eye', who has thought about the matter too much and is confused and uncertain now, while the marching men have no doubts at all about doing the right thing. It is a 'patriotic' poem in the sense in which the word was understood in the early years of the war.

NOTES AND GLOSSARY:

Leaving all ... win us: leaving all that could keep us here, all that we
   hold dear
purblind: nearly blind
Dalliers: triflers, idlers
England's need are we: we are what England needs (Hardy's highly
   individual diction is at times difficult to understand).
   Readers may recall here Kitchener's famous 'Your
   country needs *you*' poster which seems to echo
   Hardy's poem
braggarts: boastful bullies, i.e. the Germans

In Time of 'The Breaking of Nations' (1915) (G/C/O)

This is a timeless picture of peace: a man is working in the field, getting it ready for sowing (an image of future prosperity), a heap of weeds is smouldering by the field. Such actions will always go on while kings come and go, nations rise and fall. A pair of lovers walks by: the story of love such as theirs will live forever while wars will be forgotten.

Written in 1915, this is one of Hardy's outstanding poems. It consists of three small pictures (not unlike the tiny drawings in a medieval Book of Hours recording actions which will go on forever while battles and wars fade and are forgotten. The effect is partly reassurance, that life will go on and that the war will not last forever, but partly also an assertion that in the history of man across the centuries wars soon lose their importance and pass into oblivion. This second message is harder to accept as it carries with it the implicit declaration that all the lives lost in the war will have been wasted. Like the characters in Hardy's novels, the war dead have been the gods' playthings, thrown away without pity.

NOTES AND GLOSSARY:

stalk: walk stiffly (an odd choice for the image, clearly dictated by the exigencies of rhyme)

'The Breaking of Nations': from a passage in the Bible, Jeremiah 51:20, 'With thee will I break in pieces the nations', threatening the enemies of Israel with total destruction

harrowing clods: breaking up clods of earth with a harrow, a spiked metal frame pulled by a horse

couch-grass: a kind of weed

Dynasties: successions of kings from the same families

wight: (*archaic*) man

Rudyard Kipling (1865–1936)

Kipling was born in Bombay, the son of the principal of the Lahore School of Art. He was educated in England, at Haileybury School (then the United Services College) and returned to India to work as a journalist. After the success of his volume of poems and two collections of short stories he returned to London in 1889 and settled in London. Except for an extended visit to his American wife's Vermont home he remained in England, pursuing his highly successful literary career as the author of such works as *Barrack Room Ballads* (1892), *The Jungle Books* (1894–5), *Kim* (1901), *Just So Stories* (1902). In 1907 he was awarded the Nobel Prize for Literature, and he refused the Poet Laureateship three times.

His only son John, a lieutenant in the Irish Guards, was killed in action in 1915. The blow was all the more severe because John was too young to join the army, and was only able to do so through his father's influence. Those who think of Kipling as a jingoist, imperialist warmonger should read his bitter 'Epitaphs of War'.

Kipling was perhaps too easily seduced by popular slogans, and lacked the ability to grasp wider issues ahead of others, but he was a brilliant craftsman in verse and is worth studying as a spokesman for the many, especially for the ordinary soldier (with all the weaknesses which that implies). For many years he contributed to the Last Post being sounded at the Menin Gate Memorial, Ypres, a gesture which may be regarded as a piece of sentimentality or as an expression of his need to remember, and to warn perhaps.

Dirge of Dead Sisters (1902) (*M*)

As the poem's subtitle makes clear, this is an emotional tribute to the nurses who died during the Boer War (1899–1902). Stanza by stanza the poet records their quiet heroism and their steady devotion to duty, and their death of disease and exhaustion. The relentless beat of the lines recalls the harsh routine of their daily lives. Each alternate stanza asks a question, and the stanzas in between supply an answer or a gloss on the question. The method is dramatically effective, and was much used by Kipling. The full text of this poem may be found in *The Works of Rudyard Kipling*, Wordsworth Editions, Ware, 1994, p. 218.

NOTES AND GLOSSARY:

the meaner years: the humdrum years, not ennobled by war sacrifices
abutment: junction of an arch to its support
Maxim: type of automatic machine-gun
flagless: normally the coffin of a serving soldier was covered by the Union Jack
firing-party: a round of gunfire was fired at the grave as a salute to the dead
so light to lower down: that is, to lower into the grave
the Waiting Angel: the recording angel who will be present at the Day of Judgment
Uitvlugt, Simon's Town: towns in South Africa; the latter is a naval base near the tip of the Cape of Good Hope
Her that fell: Mary Kingsley (1862–1900), niece of the author Charles Kingsley. She travelled in West Africa and left excellent accounts of her travels (for instance *Traveller in West Africa*). During the Boer War she served as a nurse and died nursing Boer prisoners

The Hyaenas (*M*)

A poem inspired by the Boer War again, it is a parable of those who profit by the war: like the hyenas they are living on the dead. The poem is partly directed against those who abuse the dead because they had fallen in what many people regarded at the time, with good reason, as an unjust war.

The first, fifth and sixth stanzas are vivid cameos of the Boer War – the haste with which the dead are buried in the fierce heat, the hyenas digging out the corpse, tugging at his army shirt. The dead man's face is seen briefly for the last time before the animals close in. It is a 'pitiful face', appealing for our compassion, but the poet feels not only pity but anger as well, directed against those who abuse the dead. Here as elsewhere Kipling is not concerned with the rights and wrongs of a war, but with the fate of the ordinary soldiers who died fighting the war.

NOTES AND GLOSSARY:
burial-parties: soldiers detailed to bury the dead after battle
the baffled kites: the kites cannot savage the buried bodies
snout: push with their snouts
tushes: tusks, teeth

Charlotte Mew (1869–1928)

Born in Bloomsbury into a comfortable middle-class family (her father was an architect), Charlotte Mew was educated at the Lucy Harrison School for Girls, also in Bloomsbury. After her father's early death the family found itself in considerable financial difficulties. Charlotte had some success with her short stories and articles early in her writing career, and started writing poetry only later. Oppressed by poverty and ill-health, she lacked confidence in her own ability, in spite of having been awarded a Civil List pension on the recommendation of Thomas Hardy, John Masefield and Walter de la Mare. A tiny, eccentric woman, usually dressed in men's clothes, she was seen occasionally at Harold Monro's Poetry Bookshop. When her beloved sister died in 1928, Charlotte Mew took her own life.

The Cenotaph (September 1919) (C/R)

Charlotte Mew's poem sums up the mood of many after the war: far from being a land fit for heroes, England had little to offer to the returning soldiers. It seems that no preparations had been made, or even thought of, for coping with the flood of men discharged from the army. There was, understandably, anger and bitterness, here expressed by a woman.

In some ways the poem is unusual, shifting its theme from mourning the young dead to indignation at the profitable trafficking that goes on while the dead are forgotten. There is a poem on the Cenotaph by Kipling, 'London Stone. Nov. 11, 1923', which offers an interesting contrast to Charlotte Mew's poem. There is no doubt about the sincerity of Kipling's grief, but for once the skill with which he wrote his lines betrayed him, and the repetition of 'grieving' is ineffective. What is moving is the author's discovery that sharing his grief with others who stand there like he, mourning, will ease his pain. Yet Charlotte Mew, who suffered no such personal loss in the war, gets nearer the heart of the matter – the desolation of loss, the sense of waste, the horror at the destruction of young bodies. Ivor Gurney's 'To His Love' conveys similar emotions in a more anguished, raw form.

NOTES AND GLOSSARY:

Cenotaph: tomb-like monument to a person whose body is buried elsewhere; the word is for obvious reasons commonly used for monuments to the war dead

the wild sweet blood: the adjectives stress the intoxicating quality of youth

too deep a stain: too much blood had been shed on the battlefield for the soil to yield a harvest

But here ... build the Cenotaph: the poet sees a different sort of Cenotaph – one that would commemorate the agonies of those mourning for the war dead

Victory, winged: the famous statue of Nike, the winged Greek goddess of victory is referred to here. Discovered in Samothrace, the statue is now in the Louvre

From the little gardens: in deliberate contrast to the pomp of official monuments this cenotaph should be decorated with the humble flowers from the dead men's home villages

God is not mocked: see the Bible, Galatians 6:7 ('Be not deceived; God is not mocked: for whatsoever a man soweth, that shall he also reap'). To set up a monument in a public place given over to making money, is a mockery of the dead (who died for nothing, as nothing has changed). The initial perception of the war as a defensive, patriotic military action changed over the years, and the war came to be seen as a crusade for a better England (perhaps to make those huge sacrifices seem more worthwhile)

Wilfred Owen (1893–1918)

Owen was born in Oswestry, Shropshire, the son of a railway worker and of his ambitious, disappointed wife. He was educated at the Birkenhead Institute, at Shrewsbury Technical School and at the University of London. For a time he was employed as a private tutor near Bordeaux, and came under the influence of contemporary French poetry. He enlisted in 1915, becoming a second lieutenant in the Manchester Regiment, and by the end of that year he was in France. Wounded three times, he was diagnosed as suffering from shell-shock ('neurasthenia' was the euphemism used for this condition) in May 1917 and in June he was sent to the Craiglockhart War Hospital in Edinburgh.

His time at Craiglockhart was important to him both as a poet and as a man. There he met Siegfried Sassoon, sent to the hospital to silence his opposition to the war, Robert Graves and Robert Nichols, another war poet. Sassoon's influence strengthened Owen's own pacific feelings, hitherto vague, and again his influence helped Owen to express these feelings in his verse. His poetic diction too changed under Sassoon's influence, becoming simpler, more colloquial.

In October 1917, when Owen was declared fit for service again, Sassoon gave him an introduction to Robert Ross, the friend and executor of Oscar Wilde, and through Ross Owen met the novelist Arnold Bennett and the poet Osbert Sitwell, among others. He was treated as an equal ('I am held peer by the Georgians; I am a poet's poet', he wrote proudly to his mother on New Year's Eve 1917, aware that he was at last fulfilling her ambitions for him).

He was sent to Scarborough as camp commandant of the officers' quarters, which gave him time to work on his poetry. Two of his poems were published anonymously, and in January 1918 his poem on a mining disaster appeared under his name in *The Nation*.

He was more confident about his writing now, and, having left behind him his early models, Keats foremost among them, worked with enthusiasm at his innovative technique. His use of assonance and half-rhyme was noted and approved by both Graves and Charles Scott-Moncrieff (the future translator of Proust's *Remembrance of Things Past*, who too had served on the Western Front, winning the Military Cross).

In September 1918 Owen was posted back to his old battalion at the Western Front and in October he was awarded the Military Cross for gallantry. On 4 November 1918, a week before the Armistice, he was killed by machine-gun fire while leading his men across the Sambre Canal.

At the time of his death he was preparing his verse for publication, and his *Poems*, with an introduction by Sassoon, was published in 1920. By then his reputation as the finest poet of the war was secure.

Dulce Et Decorum Est (*M*/*C*/*P*/*O*)

The poem is a savage description of an incident of trench warfare, a gas attack in which one man is killed. First comes a description of the men marching wearily back to their post, too tired even to notice the thud of the gas shells exploding. So it happens that they are taken by surprise, and one man dies in the attack. We are given a horrifying description of his condition, and then comes a fierce attack on someone back in England (identified as Jessie Pope, a journalist who wrote a number of jolly patriotic poems) whose jingoist poetry is a barefaced lie: it is not sweet to die for England in this horrible manner.

Notice that Owen employs only harsh, repulsive images right from the start: the men are walking bent-kneed, coughing like old hags, cursing as they trudge through the mud, deaf and blind to the danger.

The gas attack is a nightmare in which the gasping victim, seen through the goggles of the gas mask, seems to be swimming in the thick green light, begging for the help that no one can give him.

The poem consists of four stanzas of varying length; the third stanza of only two lines is all the more emphatic for its briefness, stressing that the nightmare is still with Owen and cannot be forgotten.

We are forced to share the horror of the gassed man's agony in the fourth stanza, and are made aware of the poet's anger at what he has seen, which sharpens his tongue for the blistering attack on the patriotic hypocrisy in the last four lines.

NOTES AND GLOSSARY:

blood-shod: play on blood-shot, used of eyes: the men's feet are bleeding as they march barefoot, desperate to get away from the Front

Gas!: the Germans used mustard gas which destroyed the tissues of the lungs, with consequent internal bleeding

the clumsy helmets: gas masks

guttering: the word has two meanings, both used here: (1) threatening to go out (of a candle, here used of a man's life), and (2) gurgling like a gutter

lime: quicklime which corrodes (burns away) living tissue. The word points forward to the effect of the gas

the white eyes: the man's eyes are turning up so that only the whites can be seen

froth-corrupted: the gas destroys the lungs

My friend: Owen was apparently addressing the jingoistic poet Jessie Pope here (an earlier version of the poem was dedicated to her and others like her)

Dulce ... mori: it is sweet and proper to die for one's country. The line comes from the Latin poet Horace's (65–8BC) *Odes*, III, ii, 13

Anthem for Doomed Youth (*M/P/O*)

One of Owen's best-known poems: the stanzas are irregular in length, and pararhymes (guns – orisons; them all – their pall) are used to good effect.

In the first stanza the emphasis is on aural images: the booming guns like passing-bells, the rattle of rifle fire like hastily spoken prayers, the mad wailing of the shells as mourning choirs.

The second stanza by contrast offers quiet visual images: tearful eyes glittering like candles, girls' pale faces serving as a pall, the loving thoughts of the mourners instead of flowers. Dusk falling in English villages each night will be like the drawing of blinds, a sign of mourning.

The poet's anger is muted as his thoughts turn from the fallen men to the people back home who are left to grieve for them, the significant change of theme from the war victims to the mourners being signalled by the 'sad shires' at the end of the first stanza.

It is a poem of mourning as well as of bitter anger, and the elegiac beauty of the lines speaks of resignation and compassion. Owen wrote several drafts of this poem before he was satisfied with its form. It is worth noting his use of alliteration ('rifles' rapid rattle') to strengthen his aural images, or to pull together a line ('pallor – 'pall'). Yet the emotions which inspired the poem are so strong and genuine that there is never any question of a preoccupation with form at the expense of feeling. Recalling Owen's famous words in his draft of the introduction to his *Poems*, here indeed 'The Poetry is in the pity'. The pity he inspires in his readers is fired by the superb quality of his verse.

NOTES AND GLOSSARY:

passing-bells:	church bells rung at someone's death
orisons:	prayers
No mockeries:	no insincere funeral rites
speed them:	send them on their way
pall:	covering for a coffin. There is word-play here on 'pallor', paleness
a drawing-down of blinds:	window blinds were drawn to indicate that someone had died

Disabled (*M/C/P*)

A harrowing poem: its subject is a young soldier who had volunteered for the army even though he was still under-age. He was a handsome boy, a great athlete, popular with the girls. He joined up because it seemed the right thing to do, and he liked the uniform of the Scottish regiments. He has been invalided out, dreadfully wounded, and is now in a veterans' institution where he will remain. Legless, without arms, he sits in his wheelchair, listening to boys playing football in the park, and noticing how girls avert their eyes from him. He only wishes the nurses would take him back to his bed.

The poem plays on our feelings with ironical cross-references: the boys in the park going home to bed ('mothered') in the first stanza, and the soldier's pitiful cry in the last two lines of the poem ('Why don't they come/And put him into bed?'). The spurting blood of his terrible wounds is contrasted with the trickle of blood on his thigh after a rough game of football when he was carried in triumph by his team-mates; the cheering crowds at a match are compared to the crowds cheering the soldiers on their way to France.

The boy's simplicity of mind, his thoughtless decision to join up after a few drinks, his ignorance about the causes of the war, all are sketched in lightly, and the poem employs simple, at times colloquial language. The effect is of course all the more dramatic as we piece together the information, and try to imagine the life the boy will lead in the years ahead of him. It is a poem full of pity held back, of unspoken bitter accusations. There is no need to spell out the argument: the pity of War.

NOTES AND GLOSSARY:

his ghastly suit of grey: his hospital uniform; he had lost both legs in the war, and his arms are amputated at the elbows

mothered them: sent them home to bed

silly for his face: eager to paint him

lost his colour: lost a lot of blood

peg: either whisky or brandy and soda

kilts: worn by the Scottish regiments

jilts: flirtatious girls

daggers in plaid socks: *skean-dhu*, the dagger inserted in the knee-sock as part of the full Highland dress: the boy presumably joined a Scottish regiment

Esprit de corps: (*French*) loyalty to the body, here the regiment to which one belongs

---

The Send-Off (*P/O*)

The poem consists of iambic pentameters alternating with metrically irregular half-lines, achieving a stuttering effect, like a train in motion. It describes a night scene at a railway siding where troops are embarking on their journey to the Front. They marched in singing, their tunics decorated with flowers given to them by cheering girls along the road, but once they had boarded their train it went off almost furtively, in silence. The bystanders watching them knew nothing about them but wondered nevertheless what lay in store for these soldiers. How many of them will return? And will they come back in triumph, or, more likely, will the few lucky ones creep back silently to their country villages?

The poem is full of bitterness at the civilians' facile patriotism, contrasting it with the men's likely fate. The ultimate message is of course the wickedness of war, and pity for the soldiers' wasted lives.

NOTES AND GLOSSARY:

As men's are, dead: the soldiers' chests are decorated with flowers given to them on their march but the flowers remind the onlooker of floral tributes at a funeral

signals nodded ... to the guard: the noiseless movement of the signals and the flickering of an unsteady lamp seem to join in

	a silent conspiracy with the guard, as if the soldiers were being abducted secretly and shamefully
not ours:	not part of our regiment: the onlooker is a soldier too
mock what women meant:	mock the women's shallow patriotism
great bells:	bells pealing for victory
wild train-loads:	trains packed with cheering soldiers
Up half-known roads:	they will return as quietly as they went, back to their remote villages

Futility (*M*/*C*/*P*/*O*)

A dead soldier is lying in the sun: he was a countryman, used to rising early, at daybreak. Even at the Front he always woke early, until this snowy morning. If anything can bring him back to life it will be the sun. It brings seeds to life, many ages ago it stirred the dead planet, Earth, into life. Is it too difficult then for the sun to wake the dead man? Did the soldier grow tall and strong just to be killed like this? If such things can happen, why did the foolish sun bother to breathe life into the Earth at all?

This is a short, sad, quiet poem, as if men were whispering over the body, trying to bring it back to life. The tone, however, is not one of resignation but of rebellion: if a tall strong countryman can be killed for nothing, what was the point of giving him life in the first place? ('Was it for this the clay grew tall?')

The half-rhymes (sun – unsown; seeds – sides) are less emphatic than in 'Strange Meeting', in keeping with the quieter tone of the poem.

The use of a shorter first and last line in each stanza (three iambic feet as against four) is intriguing and doubtless deliberate: the shorter lines come closer to ordinary speech, and reinforce the impression of men talking among themselves in hushed tones.

NOTES AND GLOSSARY:

fields unsown:	fields waiting to be sown, work to be done
the clays of a cold star:	the Earth
the clay:	man, fashioned by God out of the dust of the ground (see the Bible, Genesis 2:7)

Strange Meeting (*C*/*P*/*O*)

Critics have pointed out the literary sources of this poem (Dante's *Inferno*, Shelley's *Revolt of Islam*, Canto V, xiii, 'Laon and Cythna' –

> And one whose spear had pierced me, leaned beside,
>   With quivering lips and humid eyes – and all
> Seemed like some brothers on a journey wide
>   Gone forth, whom now strange meeting did befall)

but, though the title of Owen's poem seems a borrowing from Shelley, these literary parallels are largely irrelevant to our reading of this, probably the greatest of all war poems.

The speaker, a soldier, has escaped from the battle down a huge tunnel full of sleeping men. He stirs up one of them who leaps up and stares at him with a smile of recognition. The soldier suddenly realises that they are all in Hell, but far from the battle. He speaks comfortingly to the man who answers as if for both of them, mourning the waste of their lives. Had they lived, they might have contributed much to the betterment of mankind, might have warned of the pitiful waste of war. Now, no one will heed them, wars will go on. They were ready for sacrifice, but not to be thrown away like this in a war. The speaker had recognised the soldier by his frown as the man who killed him the day before, frowning in just the same way when he bayoneted him. They were enemies then, but now it is time to sleep.

Owen took great pains over 'Strange Meeting', and we are fortunate indeed that the manuscript version, with the author's revisions and emendations, has survived, giving us a rare chance to see the poet at work. (The manuscript version, with the revisions, can be found, for instance, in Jon Silkin's *Penguin Book of First World War Poetry*, and in Blunden's edition of Owen's *Poems*.)

The poem is probably unfinished, but the abrupt ending can hardly be improved on for dramatic effect. The power of the poem lies first of all in the great image of the tunnel filled with sleeping men. There are legends of sleeping warriors in most cultures (in English literature we possess of course the legend of King Arthur and his knights), and we respond to them, and are prepared for the realisation that all those in the tunnel are dead and in Hell.

The man who faces the speaker, his enemy, is also his reflection in a mirror, as he speaks for them both (and indeed for all the war dead). The *Doppelgänger*, one's reflection in a mirror, is another image of great power, and here it is used in an entirely new way. The man and his reflection are the man and his enemy, both equally the victims of the war, both with the same thoughts and feelings. The *Doppelgänger* theme is therefore used to stress their common humanity, to reinforce the poet's message of the folly of war: in killing your enemy you are killing yourself.

The echoing of voices in the great tunnel is stressed, probably deliberately, by the half-rhymes which Owen uses with great skill in the poem. Half-rhymes, or imperfect rhymes (escaped – scooped, groined – groaned) had been used by other poets, notably Henry Vaughan in the seventeenth century, and Gerard Manley Hopkins and Emily Dickinson in the nineteenth, but there are grounds for doubting if Owen had read any of them. It seems most likely that he worked out the half-rhymes for himself (after all he was a very painstaking practitioner of his craft). Perhaps his aim was to enhance the mysterious dreamy, echoing quality of his poem; or perhaps, as has been suggested, the absence of the expected rhyme causes the reader to feel uneasy, disturbed, and thus more receptive to the verse.

We can only join the speaker in the poem in his lament at the waste of lives: if Owen had lived he surely would have gone on perfecting his craft, giving us more and greater poetry still.

NOTES AND GLOSSARY:

titanic wars: in Greek mythology the wars between the older gods, the Titans, and Zeus and his brothers and sisters, the Olympians, in which the latter were the victors. No doubt to Owen the world war was a titanic war indeed

groined: vaulted

fast: fast asleep

grained: marked in lines

braided hair: the beauty of women

cess: tax, i.e. the extortionate demands of the war. (There may be a hint here at 'cesspool', a pit in which filthy water – or blood – collects.)

parried: turned aside a blow

Jessie Pope (1868–1941)

Born in Leicester, educated at Craven House School, Leicester, and at the North London Collegiate School. A working journalist, she wrote poems, articles and fiction for popular magazines and newspapers, and was a regular contributor to the now defunct humorous weekly, *Punch*. She also edited Robert Tressell's classic of working-class lives, *The Ragged-Trousered Philanthropists*. She married Edward Babington Lenton and lived near Great Yarmouth. Altogether she published three volumes of war poetry, *War Poems* (1915), *More War Poems* (1916) and *Simple Rhymes for Stirring Times* (1916) which are characterised by a hearty, facile, at times quite offensive patriotism. The last four lines of Owen's 'Dulce Et Decorum Est' are addressed to her.

Who's for the Game? (*M*)

A piece of crude war propaganda that is truly hard to accept now. It was included in Jessie Pope's *Simple Rhymes for Stirring Times*, published in 1916, at the start of the great battles that were to cost so many lives and sicken so many people. The slangy cheerfulness is designed to appeal, but to us now it rings hollow, and it is hard to understand how it could have been acceptable even in 1916. It certainly throws a clear light on the jingoist mood prevalent in England in the early years of the war. Her line 'Who would much rather come back with a crutch' calls for a comparison with, say, Owen's 'Disabled', and goes a long way to explain his attack on the author of such verse. A short poem by another woman, Margaret Postgate Cole's 'The Veteran' (1916) goes some way to redress the balance.

NOTES AND GLOSSARY:

the game: the game of rugby and at the same time also the game of war; the parallel is maintained throughout the poem

the show: a popular slang term for the war

it won't be a picnic: it won't be easy

Herbert Read (1893–1968)

Born in Yorkshire, the son of a brewer, he was educated at Crossley's School, Halifax, and the University of Leeds. He was commissioned in the Yorkshire Regiment (the Green Howards) in 1915, and saw four years of active service (promoted to captain in 1917, winning a D.S.O. (Distinguished Service Order) in 1918, as well as a mention in dispatches). In 1919 he left the army to join the Treasury as a civil servant. Later he became assistant keeper at the Victoria and Albert Museum in London, and from 1931 to 1937 was Professor of Fine Art in the University of Edinburgh, becoming the foremost art critic of his generation as well as a poet. In 1953 he was knighted, and in 1966 he received the Dutch Erasmus Prize awarded for contribution to European culture.

His war poetry (*Naked Warriors* (1919) and Eclogues (1919)) is marked by the brutality of its images, and he wrote his best war poem ('To a Conscript of 1940') at a time when most of his fellow poets of the First World War were already dead.

His prose memoir of the war, *In Retreat*, describing the British retreat from the last major German offensive in 1918 conveys an extraordinary sense of immediacy in its short, bare descriptive sentences.

A Short Poem for Armistice Day (P)

The poem is addressed to an eminent visitor at a home for war veterans. The speaker is one of four men, each mutilated by the war in a different way, who are employed in the workshop there, making paper poppies to be sold in aid of men like themselves on Armistice Day (a custom still kept up today, though not so enthusiastically supported as in former years). The men's lives, however damaged, are not over yet, as they work clumsily on the paper flowers for buttonholes. In a light-hearted moment the speaker stuck a poppy in a candlestick, as he toiled at his task. These flowers will not fade, while men like themselves had been cut and are withering.

Read wrote this poem after the war when he became one of the Imagist poets (like Aldington). It is very different indeed in style (though not perhaps in spirit) from the work of his fellow poets of the war. At times the lines are disjointed, and only rarely do they rhyme. There is no punctuation except for the full-stops dividing the poem into regular four-line stanzas. Clearly Read followed the post-war trends of deliberately challenging the traditions of English poetry. We may remember here Owen's half-rhymes and assonances in 'Strange Meeting', which were used with great care and deliberation (as shown by the revised drafts of the poem) to enhance and strengthen the poem, and not merely to strengthen a theory of poetry. Read's poem too has the power to move us, nevertheless, particularly in the repeated sad line 'I have no power therefore have patience'.

NOTES AND GLOSSARY:

multiplying four digestions: considering four living men
a syncopated sick heart-beat: maimed as they are, they are all four still alive
lustre: gloss, shine
no increase: no gain
No seed: the paper flowers are sterile, like these men's lives

Isaac Rosenberg (1890–1918)

Born in Bristol, he was the son of poor Jewish immigrants who came originally from Lithuania. The family moved to the East End of London when Rosenberg was nine years old. They were, and always remained, desperately poor, largely dependent on Jewish charities. The boy was educated at the local Board School where his gifts for drawing and writing attracted the teachers' attention, and he was allowed to concentrate on these two subjects. He left school at fourteen, and friends helped him to go to the Slade School of Art (1911–14). While still at the Slade he exhibited his paintings at the Whitechapel Art Gallery, and had a volume of verse published (*Night and Day*, 1912).

He was encouraged in his writing by Laurence Binyon (1869–1943), later to become one of the war poets, and by Edward Marsh (1872–1953), though it is doubtful whether Marsh's influence was entirely beneficial. Inevitably the Georgian patron of arts was baffled by Rosenberg's verse and tried to direct his creative energies into more conventional channels.

In 1914 Rosenberg went to South Africa on a visit to his sister and also for the sake of his weak lungs, but he returned a year later, and a few months after his return he enlisted, and ended up in the King's Own Royal Lancaster Regiment. He enlisted not for any patriotic reasons (if anything, Rosenberg was a pacifist) but simply so that his mother would receive a separation allowance.

Early in 1916 he was sent to France, and though unfit for active service in every way (he was small, sickly, clumsy, and hopelessly absentminded) he survived until 1918. On 1 April 1918 he was killed in action – the date, All Fools' Day, seems to underline the waste of his life.

He is regarded by many as second only to Owen as a poet of the war. The two men were utter opposites: while Owen was racked by pity and oppressed by the burden of his responsibility for his men, Rosenberg remained detached, recording even the most horrendous details with a painter's judicious eye (see for instance his 'Dead Man's Dump', perhaps the most shattering poem to come out of the war).

On Receiving News of the War (C/P/O)

Though this is a country where the sun shines all the year round (South Africa), yet it shares in the coldness and wickedness of the world, of all men's hearts. With the coming of the war God suffers again, mourning for the dead as for his own children. The curse of murder is upon mankind, destroying everything.

The poem requires careful reading (Rosenberg knew that his poems were difficult, and in a letter of 1915 to Marsh he says 'for God's sake! don't say they're obscure'). Yet the message is clear: man's cruelty is destroying the world, and God watches and suffers helplessly. (We should remember that Rosenberg came from an Orthodox, deeply devout family in which God was a living presence.) The stanzas are short, the rhymes regular, and each short line is charged with meaning. There is exceptional beauty in the first stanza with its arresting opening line, but the mood darkens almost at once. There is frosty coldness on men's hearts; they have been cursed with wickedness, and their cruelty to one another torments God, as it has done since the days of Cain (Old Testament images come easily to Rosenberg). Perhaps the war will bring back purity to the world.

NOTES AND GLOSSARY:

a strange white word: we are reminded that the poem was written in South Africa, a long way from the war

No ice ... Winter's cost: neither the flowers nor the birds have been made to suffer by the harshness of the Northern winter

ice and frost and snow: a metaphor of man's unfeeling cruelty to other men

ancient crimson curse: the curse of Cain, murder (see the Bible, Genesis 6:8–15)

Soldier: Twentieth Century (C/P)

This curious poem, prophetic in some ways, is a song of praise and admiration for the soldier of the modern age. Without him Napoleon and Caesar could never have achieved their eminence. Out of his suffering came victories and conquests, the all-powerful dictators owe everything to him. Let them beware, though, the soldier is no longer just passive cannon-fodder.

Most of Rosenberg's earlier poems are cerebral rather than descriptive; oddly for such a gifted painter, he uses few visual images here.

NOTES AND GLOSSARY:

Titan: one of the giants, older gods of Greek mythology. The word is used loosely, to indicate someone of gigantic stature and power

Napoleon, Caesar: great military commanders who were powerful dictators as well

Cruel men: dictators

stolen the sun's power: an oblique reference to another Greek myth, that of Prometheus, the Titan who stole fire from heaven for the benefit of mankind

pallid days: days of weakness

Circe's swine: in Homer's *Odyssey* Circe was a witch who turned Ulysses' men into swine, a parable of degrading self-indulgence

Marching (As Seen from the Left File) (P)

Like most of Rosenberg's poems, this is a short piece, compressing its meaning into sixteen short lines. The first stanza is purely visual: the line of sunburnt necks, the red hands swinging across the khaki uniforms, the feet moving automatically in step.

The second stanza, however, goes beyond the precisely observed actuality: the marching soldiers carry on the old tradition of their regiment. Mars, the Roman god of war, still rules, but new, subtler means of killing have been devised, and death is now unleashed at a distance (through gunfire and bombs), killing strong young men at random. The soldiers are observed with a kindly eye, but the pacifist poet remembers that they are destined to die by new, more efficient means.

NOTES AND GLOSSARY:

ruddy: sunburnt to a brick red

flaming pendulums: the sunburnt arms swinging

Mustard-coloured khaki: there may be an oblique reference here to the

mustard gas, justly regarded with peculiar horror by
the soldiers

husband: preserve carefully

the forge of Mars: Mars, the Roman god of war, was the patron of black-
smiths

Blind fingers: men who do not know what they are doing, who aim
from a distance, at random

immortal darkness: death

Break of Day in the Trenches (*C*/*P*/*O*)

There are touches of humour in this poem: the cheerful grinning rat (we
may remember here the mice in Blunden's 'Third Ypres' who 'calmed
[him], on these depended [his] salvation'); the poppy, a little dusty,
which Rosenberg sticks behind his ear. The rat with his 'cosmopolitan
sympathies', equally happy in an English trench as in a German one,
serves to underline the stupidity of this pointless war. The poppy bears
another message: grown out of soil saturated with blood, it is a grim
reminder of all the deaths this stupid war has brought about. The vivid
snapshot of a soldier with a poppy behind his ear, smiling at a rat, thus
conveys a trenchant message.

NOTES AND GLOSSARY:

druid Time: break of day when the ancient druidic ceremonies
used to take place

parapet's poppy: for a full explanation of the symbolic significance of
the poppies growing in the trenches, see below, the
gloss for 'in man's veins'

the sleeping green: a curiously pastoral description of the no man's land

Less chanced: having less of a chance

Bonds to . . . murder: at the mercy of a blind murderous fate

in man's veins: there was an understandable almost superstitious
belief among the soldiers that the Flanders poppies
owed their brilliant scarlet to all the blood shed there.
In December 1915 *Punch* published a poem, 'In
Flanders Fields' by John McCrae (1872–1918), a
Canadian medical officer, which became a symbol of
the war, and particularly of the soldiers' sacrifice

Just a little . . . dust: small detail observed by Rosenberg the painter

---

Returning, We Hear the Larks (*C*/*P*/*O*)

The men are returning from patrol to their bivouac. Though relieved to
have survived the patrol, they are still apprehensive, on the alert for a gas

attack. Instead, they suddenly hear larksong in the dark where danger lurks usually.

In the midst of dreadful danger the soldiers are delighted to hear the larks instead of the expected whistle of the gas shells. Yet the danger is still there, hidden behind the beauty of the birdsong. The men listen to the birds, forgetful of the danger lurking in the dark, like a blind man dreaming on the beach, heedless of the incoming tide, or a girl delighting in her beautiful hair which may lead to her seduction and ruin.

By conventional standards this beautiful little poem is irregular in form, yet it is an accomplished, carefully wrought piece. The first two short three-line stanzas concentrate on the hidden dangers, the misery of the men's lives, into which in the next, equally short stanza joy erupts at hearing the larks. It might have just as easily been the gas shells, and danger is present still, treacherous in the dark. Again, surprisingly for a painter, the images are those of the mind rather than the eye.

NOTES AND GLOSSARY:

we have our lives: we are alive still
poison-blasted track: the line of attack by gas shells
a serpent: a reference to the Fall of Adam and Eve, brought about by Satan disguised as a serpent

---

Dead Man's Dump (C/P/O)

Rated as one of the best poems to come out of the war, 'Dead Man's Dump' lives up to its ugly title. There is a deliberate harshness, a parade of callousness almost, obliquely accusing and defiant.

The images are harsh too – the rolls of barbed wire like crowns of thorns (the biblical reference is of course deliberate, the dying soldiers re-enacting the suffering of Christ); the bodies – like empty sacks – thrown down on the ground. The carts roll over the dead bodies from earlier battles, Englishmen and Germans all lying together, testifying to the futility of war. Earth has received them greedily, yet no one saw them die, for the battle survivors are wrapped in their own horrors.

Stretcher-bearers go stumbling past with the wounded. If one of them dies, he is left with the earlier dead with their blackened decaying faces.

One dying man lay in the road and, hearing the creaking of the wheels, called out for help with his last breath. The carts reached him just as he died, and the wheels went over his face.

The whole poem is a continuous howl of horror, an accusing shriek. As the dreadful images pile up they all spell out the same message – the wickedness, cruelty and folly of war.

Stanzas Seven and Eight are a frighteningly real description of the chaos and dark terror of battle, with the images rushing past relentlessly. The elegiac note of the following stanzas is submerged in the ghastly descriptions of the decaying dead, of the carts rolling over them. The last two stanzas, recording the death of a wounded man lying in the road, is almost unbearable. There is some pity for the man, but still the wheels go over his face: he is dead, after all. The brutality of war, and what it does to the men caught in it, has never been shown so clearly.

NOTES AND GLOSSARY:

limbers: detachable front parts of gun-carriages, here used as carts to carry supplies of barbed wire
shells go crying: remember here Owen's 'choirs of wailing shells'
Fretting . . . decay: eager for them to die
soul's sack: dead body
God-ancestralled: God-given
ichor: in classical mythology the divine liquid flowing through the veins of the gods
blood-dazed intelligence: consciousness slipping away in death

Siegfried Sassoon (1886–1967)

Born in Kent into a wealthy aristocratic family, Sassoon was educated at Marlborough School and Clare College, Cambridge. He left without taking a degree and devoted himself to his two passions, cricket and hunting. Two days before the war broke out he enlisted as a trooper in the Sussex Yeomanry, and by 1915 he was commissioned in the Royal Welch Fusiliers (though not in Graves's battalion).

In 1916 he was awarded the Military Cross for exceptional bravery. Invalided out with trench fever in August 1916, he returned to France in February 1917, rejoining his battalion in the RWF. In April he was wounded and sent to hospital in England. (In May of that year his first book of verse, *The Old Huntsman*, was published.)

Increasingly troubled by the senseless continuation of the war, Sassoon sent an anti-war statement to his commanding officer in July 1917. It was read out in the House of Commons and reprinted in *The Times* the following day. With Graves acting as his witness before the medical board, Sassoon was declared shell-shocked and sent to the Craiglockhart War Hospital in Edinburgh – a convenient way of silencing an awkward war hero. At Craiglockhart he met Wilfred Owen to whom he gave much encouragement in writing and also in expressing his horror of the war.

Declared fit for duty Sassoon was sent back to France; in July 1918 he was wounded again and sent back to England, and eventually retired from the army. By this time he was the leading war poet and hero of the anti-war faction. He became the literary editor of the *Daily Herald*, published his *War Poems* (1928) and wrote his fictionalised autobiographical trilogy, *The Memoirs of a Fox-Hunting Man* (1929), *Memoirs of an Infantry Officer* (1930) and *Sherston's Progress* (1936), which contributed to his literary reputation at least as much as his poetry. In 1951 he was awarded the C.B.E., and in 1957 he was received into the Roman Catholic Church.

Absolution (*C*)

The theme of the poem is the brotherhood of the soldiers which transcends the terror and pain of war. There is an almost religious fervour in the lines, emphasised by the title and by the image of the war as a scourge, a penitent's whip. Having passed through pain and fear, the soldiers are granted absolution and peace of mind. They accept the passing of life, happy in their fellowship. These are sentiments which, genuine as they were then, the later Sassoon, implacable in his opposition to the war, would have rejected.

NOTES AND GLOSSARY:
absolution: in religous terms forgiveness of sins after confession and repentance

The General (*M/C/O*)

Sassoon's dislike of the General Staff grew with his deepening awareness of the huge losses in a seemingly endless war. He blamed the incompetence and callousness of those in charge for these losses.

The last line of the poem says it all; for all his bonhomie the General's incompetence and his willingness to sacrifice his men in an ill-conceived battle plan brought about the death of thousands.

NOTES AND GLOSSARY:
the line: the line of battle
card: funny person
Arras: scene of a 1917 battle which resulted in huge casualties
did for them: brought about their death

Base Details (*M/C/P*)

Thematically this poem is similar to 'The General'; here Sassoon vents his dislike of the base officers, eating and drinking comfortably behind the lines, well out of danger. During their drinking they have a few pitying words to say about the dead young officers, obviously of the same class as themselves ('I used to know his father well'), but really they do not care at all, and once the war is over they will return to England and live on happily.

The dislike of the General Staff was fairly universal: they were hated by the Front line officers for their supercilious, uncaring attitude, their incompetence, their arrogance. (It is now more or less accepted that the appallingly high casualties could have been avoided. Certainly by the Second World War the attitude towards the loss of lives – among the Western Allies at any rate – had changed to some extent at least. It is known, for instance, that on several occasions General Montgomery refused to take a line of attack that would have cost too many lives.)

Though neither of these short poems is great poetry, they are sharp, epigrammatic condemnations of the leadership of the war, effective as much for their wit as for the author's sincere indignation.

NOTES AND GLOSSARY:

scarlet:	red-faced, and also dressed in scarlet tunics
Base:	regimental headquarters, well to the rear of the battle line and therefore quite safe
Roll of Honour:	casualty list
scrap:	the slang word denigrates the carnage
Base Details:	pun on 'base' also meaning dishonourable

Lamentations (P)

The poem, written in 1917, records a real-life incident later described by Sassoon (under his pseudonym of George Sherston) in his *Memoirs of an Infantry Officer* (1930). Coming back to the base, Sassoon finds a half-naked soldier on the guard-room floor, howling in the madness of his grief for his brother, while a sergeant watches him silently. In the striking last two lines of the poem the author employs ironically the stiff diction of an officer and a gentleman, disapproving of such a lamentable absence of proper patriotic feelings.

In the prose version, written some thirteen years later, the sergeant speaks of the raving man with pity and understanding. It is his third time at the Front, and he has been wounded twice. Clearly his mind was already giving way even before the news of his brother's death, as he was at the time under detention for assaulting the military police.

While 'Lamentations' closes ironically with the officer's disapproval of such unpatriotic behaviour, in the *Memoirs* the author takes the incident quite calmly. 'Well, well, this is a damned depressing spot to arrive at!' he muses, munching a bit of chocolate.

The comparison is interesting but puzzling. With the passage of time bitter indignation has given way to philosophical acceptance, and the writer no longer feels the need to use irony to underline the officer's refusal to accept and honour an extreme form of grief. Or has he forgotten how he had felt?

NOTES AND GLOSSARY:

blind darkness: night too dark to see
gone west: been killed
bleeding: conventional euphemism for 'bloody'

Does it Matter? (M/P)

A short poem imbued with great bitterness against the glib words of comfort offered to the mutilated victims of the war.

If you have lost your legs, people will always be kind, and you do not have to show that you mind not being able to hunt any more. If you are blind, there are places that will train you for 'splendid work' (it was usually basket-weaving or something of that sort). And if your mind is permanently affected by the horrors you have been through, you can drink to forget and people won't mind your behaving badly.

The ironic tone of these lines has the curious effect of distancing the reader from these men's great suffering, perhaps because the author seems more concerned with the hypocritical comforters than with the victims themselves. (A useful comparison could be made with Owen's 'Disabled' in which the poet enters the young man's mind in a concentrated act of empathy. The aims are different, and so are the poems.)

NOTES AND GLOSSARY:

muffins and eggs: the traditional huge hunting tea; Sassoon 'the fox-hunting man' of course knew all about the delights of hunting
sit on the terrace: by implication, in a veterans' home
the pit: hell

Glory of Women (C/P/O)

In this anti-war poem Sassoon chooses for his target the young women of England, thrilled by the wounded heroes (as long as their wounds are in respectable places), clinging to the illusions of chivalry in a dirty war, working in munition factories. They have no idea of the reality of the war, cannot imagine British soldiers on the run, trampling on the faces of the dead in their panic-stricken flight.

The poem ends with an address to another woman – a German mother knitting socks for her son who is lying face down in the mud. The poem deliberately shocks British sensibilities in two ways: it mocks quite savagely the patriotic young women of England 'doing their bit' – and enjoying it – and it shows sympathy and kindness to a bereaved German mother. Throughout his later career in the army Sassoon was challenging the Establishment, hoping for a court martial that would inevitably result in uncomfortable disclosures about the real nature of the war. This threat, as much as his status as a wounded war hero, put any court martial out of the question.

NOTES AND GLOSSARY:
fondly: foolishly
laurelled: honoured for bravery
'retire': official euphemism for 'retreat'

Suicide in the Trenches (M/C)

The deceptively jaunty rhythm of this short poem with its four-foot iambic beat conceals the bitterness we associate with Sassoon's war poems. Here he remembers a young soldier, cheerful, not very bright, happy in his simple way. He broke down under the misery of the winter trenches and shot himself, and was never mentioned again (it seems that the soldiers did not like to talk about suicide – always a possibility at the back of their minds).

In the last stanza the poet turns on the empty-headed bystanders who cheer the marching soldiers, with no idea of the hell to which soldiers on their way to the Front are doomed. The poem highlights the gap between the jingoistic Home Front and the soldiers in the trenches, a theme that haunts many of Sassoon's poems. More than any other poet perhaps (apart from Owen) Sassoon reacts with bitterness to the ignorance and deliberate avoidance of the truth about the war which are to be found among the people back in England.

NOTES AND GLOSSARY:
soldier boy, soldier lads: a mockery of the jolly language employed by the British press
crumps: explosion of heavy bombs or shells

The Hero (M)

There is savage irony both in the title of the poem and in the first line ('Jack fell as he'd have wished') which is fully revealed in the second and third stanzas. Jack, much disliked as a shirker and a coward, certainly had no wish to die a hero's death, having tried every means to escape back to England.

It is interesting that Sassoon, while hating the war so deeply, still had nothing but dislike and contempt for the coward who put his comrades at risk by breaking down in a panic. There is no pity for him, though there is some compassion for his mother, tempered perhaps by the officer's dislike of her proud patriotic phrases. Again the gulf between the soldiers and the civilians is emphasised.

NOTES AND GLOSSARY:

the Brother Officer: the courtesy title for a fellow officer adds to the irony here

cold-footed: cowardly

Wicked Corner: a nasty, dangerous section of the trenches. The soldiers made up nicknames for the salient parts of their section of the trenches, perhaps in order to soften the horrors by familiarising them

---

Died of Wounds (*G/M*)

Lying in a hospital ward behind the Front line, the poet listens to the voice of a dying soldier. The nurses look after him well, moved by his miserable young face, but he does not see them because in his mind he is reliving his friend's death on the same sortie on which he himself received his mortal wound. In the morning he is gone, and his bed is occupied by a smiling soldier with a slight wound which is sure to take him back to England. The poem stresses the inevitable callousness of those going through the war; the nurses pity the boy, but they can do nothing for him and he disappears to make room for another casualty. Even the poet, listening to the dying boy's voice, finds himself speculating in which part of the Front line the boy had been shot, instead of pitying him.

NOTES AND GLOSSARY:

We'll never take it: the soldiers had been ordered to take an enemy post which is too well defended

snipe: shoot picking out their targets carefully, not shooting at random

Charles Hamilton Sorley (1895–1915)

Though of Scottish descent, Sorley spent his childhood in Cambridge where his father was a professor. Educated at Marlborough School, Sorley won a scholarship to University College, Oxford, but on leaving school he first went for six months to Germany which he liked very much. He narrowly escaped being trapped there by the outbreak of the war. On his return to England, instead of going up to Oxford he enlisted at once, was commissioned in the Suffolk Regiment and sent to France in May 1915. In October of the same year he was killed at Loos. His book of verse, *Marlborough and Other Poems*, was published posthumously in January 1916. It proved extremely popular, and was reprinted several times. Sorley's individual poetic voice and the maturity of his mind are extraordinary for one so young.

'All the hills and vales along' (*C/P/O*)

A most extraordinary war poem, it begins in a tone of apparent enthusiasm as a jolly marching song, but soon the use of the colloquial 'chaps' alerts the reader that all is not as it seems. The marching 'chaps' are marching to their death (never mind the patriotism) and earth is waiting to receive them.

Great men die, little men live, like Jesus and Barabbas, so why not sing joyfully on your way to death? Earth is indifferent to human fate, it grew the hemlock that killed Socrates, it blossomed unfeelingly round Christ's cross, and will go on blossoming when the bullets get you.

The hills and valleys echo the cheerful tramping of your marching feet, and the earth will echo with it still when you are dead, and the waiting earth has received you.

With all its apparent simplicity the poem is a sophisticated rebuke to the facile patriotism that was still prevalent in England at the time of Sorley's death. The lilting song rhythm of the poem serves to underline the irony of its message: march cheerfully to your death since the earth will receive you in her keeping.

NOTES AND GLOSSARY:

Barabbas: the condemned thief who was chosen by the Jews to be released instead of Jesus who was crucified (see the Bible, Matthew 27:15–23)

Socrates: the Athenian philosopher Socrates (469–399BC), unpopular for his unflinching honesty, was condemned to death on the charge of introducing new gods and corrupting the young. He was given a cup of hemlock to drink, a common way of carrying out the death penalty in ancient Athens

'When you see the millions of the mouthless dead' (*C/P/O*)

As clear-seeing as Sorley's 'All the hills and vales along', this poem is a passionate rejection of the sentimental glorification of the dead. If you see the war dead in your dreams, do not praise them, as they cannot hear; do not weep for them, as they cannot see your tears. All you can say is 'They are dead', and add that better men had died before them. If you imagine that you see the face of someone you know in that great multitude, do not

be deceived: death has taken them all, there is no one you know among
these ghosts.

This dry-eyed realism is truly shattering, offering no comfort for the
dying or for the mourners. All we are left with is an acute awareness of the
loss of a poetic voice so clear and so wise. Twenty years old when he
died, Sorley would surely have become a major figure in English letters,
combining a sharp critical intelligence with a gift for poetry.

NOTES AND GLOSSARY:

mouthless: silent
It is easy to be dead: a devastating comment on all war heroics, unex-
            peted in the early years of the war
spook: ghost

Edward Thomas (1878–1917)

Born in London of Welsh parents, Thomas was educated at St Paul's
School and at Lincoln College, Oxford. He married while still an undergraduate, and his wife Helen proved an invaluable companion and support
to him and a proud guardian of his reputation after his death. He began his
literary career by writing articles, mostly for *Poetry Review*, descriptive
pieces and biographies (including the lives of Richard Jefferies and George
Borrow, both of whom he very much admired). Much of his writing was
for money, simply potboilers.

In 1914, encouraged by the American poet Robert Frost, Thomas began
to write poetry. His material circumstances were a constant source of
anxiety as he wrote for his living, but he drew strength from his wife and
friends. In 1915 he enlisted in the Artists' Rifles, and later that year he was
commissioned into the Royal Garrison Artillery. On an officer's pay he
was free of financial anxieties for the first time in his life, and his verse
reflects his new-won freedom to write what he wanted in the little time left
to him.

He went over to France on active service in March 1917 and was killed
at Arras a month later. Since his death his literary reputation has grown
steadily, although the superb quality of his verse was not fully recognised
for quite a long time, simply because he was quite wrongly classed with
the Georgian poets and dismissed as old-fashioned and therefore negli-
gible.

His poems on the English countryside have great beauty, and his war
poems – of which there are not many as, once in the army, he seems to
have concentrated on his memories of the countryside quite deliberately,
to retain his sanity – are justly famous and a popular choice for war
anthologies. The inborn melancholy of his nature accords well with the
themes of war and death.

'As the team's head brass' (*C/P/O*)

The poet, sitting on a fallen elm, watches a man ploughing the field, gradually diminishing the bright yellow patch of weedy ground. Each time the team of horses reaches the end of the field where the poet is sitting, the two men talk a little. The ploughman has not been in the war, but quite a few from the village have gone, including his friend, killed the day after he arrived at the Front. If he had not been killed, they would have moved the fallen elm together. Thomas would not have been sitting there (presumably on leave from the army), and it would have been a different world altogether, probably a better one, though how can men judge such things if they cannot see into the future?

A sharply drawn picture of an interval of peace, the ploughing team cutting down the bright patch of weeds, a couple passing by on their way to make love in the wood, the ploughman and the poet chatting disjointedly as the horses draw abreast on turning round. There is quiet understanding between the two men, the war is accepted as incomprehensible and alien to the countryside. Their talk ebbs and flows with the regular movement of the ploughing team up and down the field. The rhythm of their talk and of the ploughing stresses the quiet rhythm of the real life away from the nightmare of the war.

The strength of Thomas's poem lies in presenting a small, clear picture of the English landscape and imbuing it with the radiance of enduring truth. There is no overt protest against the war in this poem, just a quiet sadness and a belief that the life of the country will survive somehow.

The readers may notice a curious parallel between the poem and Hardy's 'In Time of "The Breaking of Nations"'. Both poems present glimpses of the countryside – a man working in the field, a patch of weeds, a pair of lovers walking by – as an assurance of life returning and continuing.

NOTES AND GLOSSARY:

the team's head brass: the brass ornaments on the horses' bridles
fallow: unploughed ground
charlock: wild mustard, a yellow-flowered weed
share: blade of the plough
screwed: went in a winding motion
out: on active service in France
If we could see all: if we could see into the future we might think the war was a good thing

A Private (*C/P*)

An epitaph on another ploughman, one who did go to France and died there. At home he used to sleep happily out of doors after a night's drinking, under one of the bushes that dot the Wiltshire downs, but always kept secret his hiding-place. Now, buried in an unmarked grave somewhere in France, he still keeps secret his sleeping-place.

NOTES AND GLOSSARY:

staid:	sober and respectable
bedmen:	bedesmen, inmates of an almshouse with duty to pray for the founder
Mrs Greenland's Hawthorn Bush:	the ploughman's joke about sleeping rough. He makes up what sounds like the name of a pub, the Hawthorn Bush, with Mrs Greenland the landlady there

Part 3

Commentary

Like another group of English poets, the seventeenth-century Meta-physicals (the term was first used by John Dryden (1631–1700) in a derogatory sense when he criticised John Donne for affecting the metaphysics, that is, employing over-ingenious, artificial and abstruse arguments in his poetic images), the poets of the First World War are mostly discussed as a group. In treating any group of poets thus, there is always a danger of creating stereotypes, inviting preconceived notions, rather than judging each author's work on its own merits. Certainly the Metaphysicals suffered in some ways: while their reputation soared after their rediscovery, their work was studied for similarities that would justify the collective term given to them.

There is, nevertheless, good reason for treating the poets of the First World War as members of a homogeneous group (we cannot call them a movement, since their concern was not the promotion of a particular type of verse but rather giving voice to a personal anguish and rage).

There are numerous similarities between these young men, quite apart from being involved in a catastrophic war. With a few exceptions (Isaac Rosenberg, Ivor Gurney, Wilfred Owen) they all came from a comfort-able middle-class or even aristocratic background. With the exception of Rosenberg and Wilfred Owen again they had all been educated at some of the best public schools in the country and they were all university educated (even if some of them, like Sassoon and Blunden, left without taking a degree, for personal not financial reasons).

The educational background which most of them shared meant in those days a shared grounding in the classics. It is interesting, and by no means unexpected, that this familiarity with classical literature may be traced more easily in the poetry written in the early years of the war. A worship of the heroes of classical Greece went well with the joyful glorification of the war which found its fullest expression in Julian Grenfell's 'Into Battle'. It is also implied in Rupert Brooke's 'Peace' where war is seen as an almost mystical purification ritual. After the Somme such poetry gradually disappears: there was no room for heroism of this kind among the mud-trodden corpses.

A case history illustrating this change is Sassoon's short, technically accomplished poem of three stanzas, 'The Kiss' (C), a hymn of praise for the bullet and the bayonet ('Sister Steel' with her 'downward darting kiss'). Later Sassoon felt compelled to offer an explanation for this poem which is so utterly at odds with the poet's later consistent, courageous opposition to the war. He began it as a technical exercise, using Anglo-Saxon words only (in this he failed, as even a glance at the poem will show you), but the final result turned out to be a celebration of the act of killing, incomprehensible to the author himself. What is noteworthy of course is that he felt obliged to explain it, almost to apologise for it later, such was the change in the climate of opinion.

One feature of these men's classical education remained, however, and that was the habit of writing poetry, which survived the traumas of trench warfare. Verse remained the preferred form, natural and acceptable, of recording experience for these young men who had been required to write Greek and Latin verse at school, pretty well as part of their curriculum.

With the exception of Gurney and again of Rosenberg (and there is a touch of irony perhaps in the fact that Rosenberg, the self-educated odd man out, produced some of the best poetry of the war), they were all commissioned officers. While examining their military careers we cannot help noticing also how many of them had been awarded high military honours for bravery in action: M.C. (Military Cross), D.S.O. (Distinguished Service Order), mentions in dispatches – a glittering array of medals.

Another tragic distinction that went with so many of them being junior officers (because of lack of military experience and their having to lead their men into battle), was how many of them were killed in action. (It was reckoned that the average life expectancy of a junior officer on the Western Front was about nine months.) Those who survived did not escape unscathed in body or mind: of the writers discussed in Section 2 above only the women and men too old for active service (Hardy, Kipling) survived unscarred, at least physically.

Themes

War

The theme that is common to the poetry written by these men is, of course, that of the war, which dominates all their work, even if at times only tangentially (as when Edward Thomas in 'As the team's head brass' watches the ploughman at work, and they talk of the war). It does not take much imagination to see that this had to be so. The Western Front was a place of such appalling horrors, of carnage on such an unprecedented scale, that anyone who went through his active service there was condemned to remember for the rest of his life what he had seen, heard and felt there.

W. B. Yeats's reasons for excluding the war poets from his 1936 anthology *The Oxford Book of Modern Verse* – 'passive suffering is not a theme for poetry' and 'If war is necessary ... it is best to forget its suffering as we do the discomfort of fever' – can now, after yet another world war and in a world that no longer expects perfect peace, only be read with astonishment and incomprehension. What of the anger and rage at the suffering witnessed? Is that a passive reaction? What of the compassion and of the love? And indeed what of the beauty remembered and cherished amid desolation? All these are noble emotions born out of that dreadful war, and it was impossible for the war poets to forget the reality that overwhelmed them. One can only assume that Yeats, engrossed in the Irish struggle, never looked beyond the Irish Sea and never really saw the drama acted out so tragically with a cast of millions. To men living then, let alone to those fighting in that dreadful war, this was a reality that could never be put aside like the memory of a fever. Owen's 'Insensibility' (*C/P/O*) is a description not of forgetting but of the painful gradual hardening of sensibilities which was the only course, and open only to some.

The war was always there but what changed was men's perception of it. The great battles of 1916 (Verdun and the Somme foremost among them) were the watershed. Whereas before these battles took place it was still possible to write of the glory of war, it was no longer possible to do so after the battles.

Charles Hamilton Sorley's was perhaps the only dissenting voice during the earlier years. Killed too early to experience the worst yet to come, he was remarkably prescient and saw the killing for what it was, a wicked folly on a monumental scale.

Rupert Brooke's immensely popular war sonnets predate, of course, the bitter fighting and so does Laurence Binyon's 'For the Fallen' (*M*) an enthusiastic tribute to the war dead, published in September 1914, well before the corpses began to pile up. (The fourth stanza of Binyon's poem became a favourite text for war memorials all over the country.) Even Siegfried Sassoon's early poetry sings of the brotherhood of the 'happy legion' in exalted terms.

The carnage of the Somme changed everything. Instead of abstract heroics the poetry grew more and more concerned with the fate of the individual soldier.

As the war advanced into its second and lasting stage of huge battles fought with enormous loss of life for relatively small territorial gains, poetry changed. It was based more and more on agonising personal experience, and concerned with individual fate. These young men saw their fellow officers and the men in their charge die horribly or survive as shattered remnants of humanity. What they saw became the subject of their poetry. The 'Millions of the mouthless dead' that Sorley foresaw became individuals whom the poets knew, perhaps liked, perhaps loved: the lad with a lovely Buckinghamshire accent in Gurney's 'The Silent One', the ploughman who liked sleeping rough in Thomas's 'A Private', the boy who killed himself in Sassoon's 'A Suicide in the Trenches'. These are all individuals whose characters are sharply defined even in the shortest poems.

The wounded and the dead

In the majority of the poems dealing with death and mutilation what comes across very strongly is the writer's readiness to share in the pain and terror, almost to accept responsibility for it. Some of this is of course the officer's awareness of being implicated in the suffering, however unwillingly, simply by obeying orders. Some of it is best described as brotherly love, the fellowship that binds men who share the same dreadful predicament; and some of it, a significant part of it, is pity, compassion, what Owen calls 'The eternal reciprocity of tears' ('Insensibility').

There are inevitably some recurring themes in such poems – watching a dying man in a hospital ward (Owen's 'Conscious' (C), Sassoon's 'The Death-Bed' (C) and 'Died of Wounds' (C)); watching a man dying on the barbed wire (Gurney's 'The Silent One', Blunden's 'Festubert: The Old German Line' (C), Graves's 'The Dead Boche'). These are images of dread, reluctantly retained in memory. They are repetitive because such dreadful things happened again and again.

There are other, quieter scenes, not the less terrible for being enacted long after the battles: Owen's 'A Terre' (C) and his 'Disabled' and 'Mental Cases' (C), Sassoon's sardonic 'Does it Matter?'.

There is one poem, 'Dead Man's Dump' by Isaac Rosenberg, to be set against all these: it is matter-of-fact in its recording of details (a dead man's brains splattering the bearer's face), and its impact is shattering, especially in the last image of the wheels of the limbers going over the face of a man who has just died. The matter-of-factness does not signal dumb acceptance, though. No one has shown more effectively the deafening madness of a shell attack ('The air is loud with death'), its impact on the survivors ('the startled blood may stop'). After the maniacal howling of the shells there follows a quiet coda: the trudging of the cars over the bodies of the fallen. There is pity in the last two stanzas, unspoken but nevertheless present in the description of the dying man's last feeble cries. What is absent is any sense of guilt, of a shared responsibility, and we may remember here that Rosenberg was a private, a man just carrying out orders. The anger is controlled by a searching intellect ('Who hurled them out? Who hurled?') but it is there, in the line about 'the half-used life' of the fallen.

To define the quality that separates Rosenberg's poem from the others we might compare it with a poem by Ivor Gurney (another private). 'To His Love', a lament for a beloved friend, starts quietly enough with recollections of happier days in the Cotswolds and on the Severn, but then the horror of death breaks in with the shriek 'Cover him, cover him soon!', cover that hideous sight which must somehow be wiped from memory.

We are aware of the anguish of seeing a beloved person die horribly. No wider meaning is sought, there are no questions of guilt and responsibility; instead there is the unbearable pain of a violent death witnessed helplessly. Rosenberg's cerebral approach, the scrutiny of a painter's sharp eye, shock by what they describe so clearly, while Gurney's poem, though it contains the one shocking picture of the bleeding mutilated corpse, makes its impact by the rising cry of anguish, almost of hysteria. Both are deeply personal reactions to the carnage.

Beyond such bloody dying is death itself. Sorley saw it as a signpost to a friendless land he wants to know, a putting away of the past ('Two Sonnets' (C/P). His 'millions of the mouthless dead' are simply dead, not to be pitied: they have gone where others had gone before. Such paring down of death is rare, however. To Rupert Brooke, in the early months of the war, death was an honourable choice, peace for sickened minds. Later, to Edward Thomas in his 'Lights Out' (C), death was a forest in which he could lose himself, a sleep.

Such abstractions of death rarely survived for long the reality of the trenches. Beyond such horrors, however, lies Owen's vision, 'the pity war distilled'. His 'Strange Meeting' is justly seen as the greatest of all war poems. The reader will always remember the vast underground tunnel filled with the sleeping dead men, and the meeting of the two enemies, both now dead. The horror of war is hinted at in the description of the moment of death but the stress is on the waste of young men who could· have done such great things. Yet the note is not elegiac, the poem reaches beyond sadness, beyond mourning to a bleak calm of despair – not the defiant despair of men facing 'dull clashing death' of Blunden's 'The Zonnebeke Road', but despair beyond all human emotion.

In the face of such despair it seems somewhat unfitting to speak of anti-war sentiments, but the theme of the futility of war rings naturally through all these poems – the futility of dying like this. It takes many forms, of course. Owen himself asks despairingly in 'Futility' why man was created at all if his striving is to end in a pointless death, while in his 'Dulce Et Decorum Est' he speaks witheringly of 'The Old Lie', that it is sweet and fitting to die for one's country. Sassoon's brief sardonic poems ('The General', 'Base Details'), Blunden's weary remembrance ('1916 seen from 1921') are all oblique comments on lives thrown away in a pointless war. The last line of Sassoon's 'To any Dead Officer' (G) ('I wish they'd killed you in a decent show') says it all.

The memory of all the deaths remains, a reluctant nightmare. In Blunden's 'Thiepval Wood' the roar of the guns will forever be heard in thunderstorms, in his 'La Quinque Rue' the peaceful post-war Flemish landscape turns into the battleground yet again in the poet's mind, just as in his '1916 seen from 1921': 'the charred stub outspeaks the living tree' – the memory of the blasted landscape of Flanders is more vivid than the English countryside the poet now inhabits. To Graves in 'Recalling War' the memory brings back a mad exhilaration, 'the duty to run mad', the childish delight in destruction, while Sassoon's war-shattered survivor in 'Repression of War Experience' (C/P) is driven mad by the roar of the guns in his head. (Recalling Rosenberg's 'Dead Man's Dump', Aldington's 'Bombardment' (G/C), Owen's 'Strange Meeting' where 'no guns thumped', the hideous cacophony of guns in his 'Anthem for Doomed Youth', we are forced to try to understand the impact of constant bombardment on the men cowering in their dugouts.)

The right and proper corollary of thoughts on death and the futility of war is anger, directed not so much at the Germans (hatred of the enemy faded as the war went on; there were corpses hanging on the barbed wire on both sides of no man's land), as at the General Staff, snug at the base, well out of danger, shifting their cannon-fodder as they worked out their plans of attack. Sassoon, the most outspoken of the war poets and the most politicised one, expressed his feelings very clearly indeed in 'The General' and 'Base Details', as did Owen in 'Dulce Et Decorum Est', 'Anthem for Doomed Youth' and of course 'Strange Meeting'. Not all of this anger was directed against the General Staff, however. The soldiers' view of the people of England underwent a profound change as the war went on, but then England itself was changing.

Keep the Home Fires Burning – the Home Front*

When the soldiers sang 'Keep the Home Fires Burning' they were celebrating a sentimental, idealised picture of England that no longer corresponded to reality. Though most women were still at home, looking after their families, an increasing number of them went out to work, largely connected directly or indirectly with the war. In 1915 there were about 50,000 women working in munition factories, but by 1917 not only were there many more women on the factory floor, but they were replacing the absent men in all kinds of work. Jessie Pope's 'War Girls' (R) offers a list of the jobs done by women – milkman, train conductor, lift operator, van driver, doorman – 'Till the khaki soldier boys come marching back'. The assumption was of course that once the war was over women would

---

*This section draws on material collected by Catherine Reilly in *Scars Upon My Heart*. The anthology is excellent, the women's poetry largely of inferior quality. Undoubtedly there is scope for an enquiry as to why this should be so.

go back to their families or to domestic service, but things did not work out quite like that. The freedom of a factory job with fixed hours and a steady wage was infinitely preferable to the subservience of a domestic servant, and so England changed, slowly but for good. As working women gained self-confidence they began to look beyond their narrow domestic concerns. That without the war the suffragette movement would have faced a much harder, much longer struggle for votes for women, is obvious. (Women in Britain gained a limited right to vote in 1918, and full voting rights in 1928.)

For middle-class women factory work was out of the question, but voluntary work – nursing, especially, as well as clerical work in the forces – was approved of and encouraged. May Wedderburn Cannan's 'Rouen' is an affectionate – and in retrospect perhaps idealised – picture of a V.A.D. nurse's work, and Rudyard Kipling's 'Dirge of Dead Sisters', though inspired by the Boer War, records the admiration that was accorded to such women.

Not only did the war bring socio-economic changes to affect people's lives, it also caused a gap to widen gradually – and this is remarkably well documented in contemporary poetry – between the soldiers and the people back home in England. While the patriotic enthusiasm of the men at the Front changed to a weary resentment and to anger, such changes were much slower at home.

Incapable of envisaging the deprivations suffered by the soldiers in the muddy trenches, the people in England did not find it incongruous to voice their petty complaints. Undoubtedly, as the German blockade of the sea made itself felt, supplies of food from overseas (on which Britain depended very considerably) dwindled alarmingly, food stocks dropping at times to a quantity sufficient for four weeks only. Rationing was piecemeal, and introduced rather late, and there was no orchestrated effort to 'Dig for Victory', i.e. grow food in Britain to feed the British.

Paradoxically, while the middle class suffered, lamenting the disappearance of the large Sunday joint ('no unpatriotic joint' in Aelfrida Tillyard's 'Invitation au Festin' (R)), mocking the Food Controller's exhortations to prepare economic dishes and dreaming of the return of Fuller's walnut cake (Margaret Postgate Cole in 'Afterwards' (R)), the working class found itself significantly better off. The war brought full employment and higher wages, especially for those in reserved occupations (munition workers and miners) and rationed food was better than starvation. (At the introduction of conscription in 1916 it was found that only three out of nine conscripts were fit for service: the rest of them were suffering from malnutrition. A glance at contemporary photographs of men lining up to be measured for their uniforms bears this out, and Emily Orr's poem 'A Recruit from the Slums' (R) is a rare admission of this sorry state of affairs.)

Of course, people's ignorance of the conditions at the Front enabled them to maintain their blind patriotism much longer. Vera Brittain in her *Testament of Youth* speaks of 'that terrible barrier of knowledge by which War cut off the men who possessed it from the women who remained in ignorance'. It was the girls who offered white feathers (the badge of cowardice) to men whom they regarded as shirkers, though to be fair there were many women who disliked such cheap gestures as much as Siegfried Sassoon did. Helen Hamilton wrote a little poem 'The Jingo-Woman' (*R*) which is not great poetry but full of good sense.

In contrast to the jingoist warmongering there were, surprisingly, some women's voices to be heard speaking out against the prevailing glorification of war. Thus Pauline Barrington in 'Education' (*R*) is as outspoken as any *Guardian*-reading mother of our time:

> If the child is father of the man,
> Is the toy gun father of the Krupps?
> > For Christ's sake think!
> > While you sew
> > Row after row.

Alice Meynell (1847–1922), a member of a renowned literary family and an established poet herself, and the novelist Mary Webb (1881–1927) both spoke out against the war as early as 1914.

Still, it was the people at home who broke the windows of shops with German-sounding names while most soldiers at the Front gradually came to take the view expressed by Edward Thomas in 'This is No Case of Petty Right or Wrong' (*G/P*):

> I hate not Germans, nor grow hot
> With love of Englishmen, to please newspapers.
> Beside my hate for one fat patriot
> My hatred of the Kaiser is true love

reserving their hatred for the incompetent General Staff.

But if the people at home remained largely ignorant of the real horrors of the trenches, they knew about the scale of the devastation from the casualty lists. As a whole generation of young men was almost wiped out, their loss left a whole generation of young women in mourning. A poignant advertisement quoted by Vera Brittain in *Testament of Youth* reads as follows: 'Lady, *fiancé* killed, will gladly marry officer totally blinded or otherwise incapacitated by the War'. (Brittain herself lost her fiancé as well as her beloved brother in the war, and in her poem 'The Superfluous Woman' – which appears in *Testament of Youth* – she speaks of the anguish of these women.)

No great poetry was written by these bereaved young women, but their gentle, sad voices may be heard in their dignified ('lady-like' is the word that springs to mind) mournful verse. It was left to Wilfred Owen to speak in a truly poetic voice of the loss suffered by the 'sad shires' in his 'Anthem for Doomed Youth'.

There was also a feeling of guilt, and perhaps of resentment, among the young women at not being able to share in the danger – as Gabrielle Elliot says sadly in 'Pierrot Goes to War'(R): 'Pierrot goes forward – but what of Pierrette?'.

Nowhere is the gap between the people at home and the men at the Front wider than in their perception of the role of religion in the war. At the beginning of the war it was still possible for Rupert Brooke to say 'Now, God be thanked Who has matched us with His hour' ('Peace'), but neither the sentiment nor the form survived into the later years of the war. It is understandable that soldiers should have been turning away from Established religion. The sight of clergymen blessing the soldiers' arms (on both sides of the no man's land) must have brought first doubt and then rejection of such travesties of Christ's teaching. Siegfried Sassoon's satirical 'They' (O) is a direct attack on the Church: 'The Bishop tells us: "When the boys come back/They will not be the same: for they'd have fought/In a just cause."'

There are poems which equate the soldiers' suffering with Christ's: 'Once more our anguished way we take/Towards our Golgotha' in Robert Nichols's 'Battery Moving up to a New Position from Rest Camp: Dawn' (C), or Sassoon's 'The Redeemer' (C) where the weary soldier with his load of planks becomes for a glimpse Christ with his burden of the cross, or Herbert Read's 'My men, my modern Christs' in 'My Company' (C). These are metaphors for suffering, not appeals to God for help and succour – or is the agonised last line of Sassoon's 'Attack' (G) ('O Jesus, make it stop!') more than routine army blasphemy?

Things were different back home, where the women turned to their religion for comfort and for justification of all the suffering. To equate the dying soldier with Christ was to give a meaning to his death; no longer senseless, it was a noble self-sacrifice, and so death acquired a purpose in the very act of dying.

Muriel Stuart's 'Forgotten Dead, I Salute You' (R) elaborates the comparison between a dying soldier and Christ into the ritual of the Last Supper: 'Eat, drink, and often as you do,/For whom he died, remember him.'

Similarly Mary H. J. Henderson's 'An Incident' (R) equates a soldier's wounded hands with the marks of the nails on Christ's hands. Christ's words (John 15:13) 'Greater love hath no man than this, that a man lay down his life for his friends' inspired Alice Meynell's 'Summer in England, 1914' (R), and without a doubt these same words comforted many of those mourning at home. Poems like Alberta Vickridge's 'In a

V.A.D. Pantry' (*R*) and Lucy Whitmell's 'Christ in Flanders' (*R*) express the same belief.

Without questioning the sincerity of these poems, they stress for us the gap between the Home Front and the soldiers in the trenches quite as much as Robert Graves's scathing comments (in *Goodbye to All That*) on the letter from 'A Little Mother' which appeared in the *Morning Post* in summer 1916, and by popular demand was reprinted as a pamphlet in a print-run of 75,000 copies. Graves's remark about 'war-madness that ran wild everywhere, looking for a pseudo-military target' seems a mild understatement after 'Little Mother's' warmongering. Such madness offers every justification for Sassoon's dislike of the patriots at home, expressed very trenchantly in his 'Glory of Women' and 'Blighters' (*G*) or for Owen's attack on Jessie Pope and her kind in 'Dulce Et Decorum Est'.

But as we have found, not all women supported the war, and Charlotte Mew's 'The Cenotaph', written less than a year after the war ended, when memories were fresh still, represents the best of the poetry of the anti-war faction at home:

> While looking into every busy whore's and huckster's face
> As they drive their bargains, is the Face
> Of God: and some young, piteous, murdered face.

'We are the happy legion' – love and friendship

Much has been written about the homosexual element in the poetry of the First World War. It seems pretty certain that Gurney and Sassoon, and perhaps Owen too, had at least some homosexual leanings, and Rupert Brooke also may have had a homosexual affair in his undergraduate days.

As Graves remarks in *Goodbye to All That*, in English public schools romance is necessarily homosexual, and the system does seem to be a training in homosexuality, not necessarily lasting into adulthood, though. Yet to explain the emotion that bound these men together purely in sexual terms is an over-simplification. Undoubtedly for outsiders it is just as difficult to understand the nature of these relationships as it is to imagine what life in the trenches really was like. We read about the shells, the gas, the mud, the lice, the cold, the endless winter rains, the constant terror, but can we really understand what it was like? The numbing of sensibilities that made men shake hands with a corpse lying in their way on the fire-step, with a cheerful 'Put it there, Billy Boy' (an incident described by Graves in *Goodbye to All That*) and that is described by Owen in his poem 'Insensibility', is impossible for an outsider to understand. The word 'outsider' is crucial here, for this was a closed society – as Graves says in 'Two Fusiliers', bound together 'by the wet bond of blood'.

The bonds were strongest between men who fought together and lived together in the enforced intimacy of the trenches. Other soldiers were regarded in an amiable manner or not, as the case may be, but though all the soldiers understood one another well enough, it was their own Company, their own Battalion that created the true bonds. In his *Undertones of War* Blunden tells of one such little unit, a trench maintenance party who kept their lodgings in a cellar neat and tidy, taking turns at cooking and cleaning. They were quiet, shy men, happy in each other's company, talking of their families – and they all died together in the same attack.

There were other bonds apart from those of friendship. Between an officer and his men there existed a relationship not unlike that of a father and his sons. It is touching and sad to think of these young officers, some of them barely in their twenties, looking after their men, fighting along them and in so many cases dying with them. Blunden in *Undertones of War* tells of a similar paternal affection bestowed on himself by his commanding officer. The young Lieutenant Blunden was variously called 'Bunny' and 'Rabbit', tactfully sheltered from the most shattering sights, and praised when a book of his verse received a favourable review in the august *Times Literary Supplement*.

Naturally the relationship between an officer and his men, or between the enlisted men and the NCOs was not always an idyllic one. Gurney's 'The Silent One' records his dislike of his officer, foolishly incompetent, with a 'finicking' voice, and Robert Graves's 'Sergeant-Major Money' (*C/O*) tells of the murder of the martinet sergeant-major by two privates. (In his *Goodbye to All That* he recounts a real-life story of two Welsh privates who murdered the Company sergeant-major by mistake, intending to kill a much hated platoon sergeant. They were both court-martialled and shot, and the incident must have inspired the poem.)

These are anecdotal instances of the vagaries of human relationships, nothing to do with the depth of affection, indeed of love, between comrades in the war.

Robert Nichols's 'Casualty' (*C*) and his 'Comrades: An Episode' (*M*) try to express that love, but there is an overwrought sensibility at work here, and the poems fail. Gurney's 'To His Love', on the other hand, has a depth of emotion that convinces and shatters; here is a man who has seen his beloved friend die, and who cannot bear the memory of the bloodied body. Reading the poem you are aware of the love and of the pain of loss where the instinct to forget the unbearable and the yearning to remember are fused.

Owen's 'Greater Love', (included in his *Collected Poems*, London, 1963), seems to reject sexual love in favour of the sacrificial love of the dying soldier. It would be a mistake to see this poem simply as a declaration of homosexuality; the title itself, surely taken from Christ's words in John 15:13 ('Greater love hath no man . . .') draws our attention to the sacrificial aspect of this love, and each stanza takes up and rejects an aspect of a woman's love, contrasting it with the agony of the dying soldier. The soldiers are described not in terms of their physical attributes, but in their pain. It seems that what Owen had witnessed in the trenches turned his thoughts away from ordinary sexual love towards an almost mystical adoration of the men who suffered and died. They died unpitied, even God seems to have forsaken them: in a God-less world their self-sacrifice approaches Godhead.

Much has been made of the misogyny of the poem, but it is a rejection of the whole concept of a sexual relationship, based on taking not giving, and there lies the point: the self-sacrifice is selfless, utterly pure. The woman's role is inevitably marginal, as historically there is no place for her in a war. The last line, echoing Christ's words to Mary Magdalene (John 20:17, 'Touch me not') relegates her to the role of a mourner (like the women of the 'sad shires' in 'Anthem for Doomed Youth'). The poem is an attempt to define the fellowship of comrades in a war, based on common experiences which cannot be described and will not be comprehended by outsiders. Men who have gone through extremities of terror together and have come out alive together, certainly know and understand each other in a unique way. The ties are emotional, not physical, and their supreme expression is self-sacrifice.

Nature

There is another major theme running through much of the work of these poets, one that is diametrically opposed to the theme of war and death. This is nature, significant enough for many of them to merit discussion here.

These poets see two different landscapes – the battle-scarred Flemish or French countryside, and the smiling English landscape they left behind. They try to keep the two images separate, for their sanity may depend on their hope that one day they will find themselves back among the English hedgerows. Yet the nightmare they have been living in has such a hold over them that they may not be able to escape. Thus for Blunden the 'Zillebeke Brook' (*C*), 'deformed with cruelty', conjures up distorted images of the Kentish landscape. Seen after the war, fully restored and neat again, 'La Quinque Rue' turns back into the old, familiar nightmare of barbed wire, sentries, ragged corpses. Back in England once more, several years after the war, the poet still does not feel at home there: 'But now what once was mine is mine no more' ('1916 seen from 1921').

Yet during the worst shell attacks it was the thought of nature, the least token of her presence – and the promise of her return to the blighted land – that maintained Blunden's sanity, as he himself admits in 'Third Ypres' (*P*) when, cowering with his friends in a concrete pillbox, he watches some field-mice ('nimble,/And tame') on whom 'depended [his] salvation', his sanity as he watches. For Blunden, who through the war held on to his belief that nature will prevail in the end and bring the desolate battlefield back to life, ironically in the years after the war this same desolate battlefield proved victorious: the survivor, mourning so many dead, cannot break free of his nightmare memories.

By contrast, Edward Thomas should perhaps not be called a war poet even though he was killed in action at Arras. He was a poet of nature, a passionate lover of the English countryside who was making his name, but not as a poet of the war. His 'Adlestrop', (included in his *Collected Poems*, Oxford, 1978), is a magical evocation of a hot June afternoon at a small station in the Cotswolds, perfect and memorable. Though the war is a crucial agent of change in his 'As the team's head brass' and a subject of serious conversation between the poet and the ploughman, the rhythm of the ploughing and the rhythm of their conversation evoke the unchanging round of the seasons, of the countryman's year. More directly concerned with the war is his brief poem 'A Private', a half-serious epitaph on a hard-drinking Wiltshire ploughman killed in France. Yet even this short poem of eight lines evokes the downs, dotted with bushes.

Thomas's passionate love of the English countryside is an essential part of his character and of his writing. Instinctively he kept the memory of it fresh in his mind during his time at the Front, and during that time he wrote no more poetry. so deeply was his inspiration bound up with his own country.

In his poems the reader is ever made aware of the sweep of the countryside, of the road winding up into the wood, with the small figures of men not dwarfed but set in their proper places, assured and accepted. It is not by chance that the action played out in 'As the team's head brass' recalls Hardy's 'In Time of "The Breaking of Nations"'. Both poems contain a reassuring promise that nature and life will endure.

Ivor Gurney loved the Gloucestershire landscape deeply; it is recorded that the present that gave him the greatest pleasure during his sad years in the asylum was an ordnance survey map of Gloucester and its environs, an inspired gift from Helen Thomas, which enabled him to trace with delight all his old walks. In 'To His Love' the Cotswolds and the Severn are painfully bound up with his memories of his dead friend, yet even in his despair he remembers the sheep that 'feed/Quietly and take no heed', an accurate memory of the country.

Unexpectedly for an East Ender from an orthodox Jewish family, Isaac Rosenberg finds delight in the rare glimpses of the world of nature found at the Front. In 'Returning, We Hear the Larks' the sense of intoxicating pleasure at hearing birdsong instead of the half-expected and feared shells comes as fresh as rain. The contrast between the world of nature and the man-made world of terror is deliberate and significant. Similarly the cheerful rat in 'Break of Day in the Trenches' represents sturdy common sense in a mad world of death, and Rosenberg's gesture of putting a poppy behind his ear to salute the creature adds to his pleasure at finding a little bit of nature in the trenches.

No discussion of the theme of nature in war poetry would be complete without a mention of Julian Grenfell's 'Into Battle' with its strange pagan identification of the warrior with the natural world, perhaps only fully comprehensible to one well versed in classical literature, though the landscape of this hymn to war is the gentle English countryside.

Imagery

That every poet has his own individual vision is made manifest in his imagery. These poets' war experiences had much in common: the mud, the cold, the lice, the ever-present danger of instant death or ghastly mutilation, the absence of any bodily comforts, the weariness, the deafening, insistent roar of the guns. The catalogue of their miseries goes on, and they all shared them. Yet the images they hammered out to convey their experiences are vastly different.

When you have read through Blunden's verse, you too will remember what he carried away with him in his mind: the tree-stumps ('Ember-black the gibbet trees' – 'Thiepval Wood' (*C*); 'the shell-chopped trees that fang the plain' – 'The Zonnebeke Road'); the rags of uniforms clinging to the barbed wire ('The grey rags fluttered on the dead' – 'Festubert: The Old German Line' (*C*); 'On the thin breastwork flutter the grey rags' – '1916 seen from 1921'). Out of these he re-creates his nightmare.

Snow and ice belong to this countryside under a low sky, with dead brambles or rusty barbed wire rattling in the wind, all symbols of death and sterility. Significantly in what is perhaps his most powerful image of death – in his 'The Midnight Skaters' – it is found lurking beneath the ice, hating the skaters through the glass of ice. It is not a war poem, but the sense of a malignant death waiting to spring is terrifyingly apposite to war, and so Jon Silkin was right to include this poem in his *Penguin Book of First World War Poetry*.

When Blunden speaks of flowers, of colours (as in 'Vlamertinghe: Passing the Château, July 1917') it is blood he is thinking of ('this red should have been duller'). Again, in '1916 seen from 1921', 'The saints in broken shrines were bright as blood'. The horror of the war overlays his vision.

It was not so with Edward Thomas. His memory of the English landscape is sharp and clear ('the plough narrowing a yellow square/Of charlock' in 'As the team's head brass' is an accurate rendering of the gradual disappearance of the patch of weedy ground under the plough). He conveys reality so accurately through a visual metaphor because he remembers so clearly what he had seen. In 'I never saw that land before' (included in his *Collected Poems*, Oxford, 1978), he writes, 'The blackthorns down along the brook/With wounds yellow as crocus'; the word 'wounds' tells of the rawness of the cuts in the wood, while 'crocus' describes well the bright yellow of blackthorn wood. Thomas is meticulous in creating his images yet the realistic description is elevated by just a word or phrase into pure poetry. An entire landscape can be transformed in his imagination, as in 'The Green Roads' (also in his *Collected Poems*). The roads leading into the forest are strewn with white feathers as if marked by someone 'To show his track. But he has never come back'. The echoes of fairy tales, of Babes in the Wood, bring magic to a real picture of the Epping Forest. Thomas took this clear vision with him to France, but kept it to himself: as was mentioned before, he wrote no poetry at the Front.

In Ivor Gurney's work the metaphor is used to utter the unutterable. Thus 'clay binds hard' in 'Butchers and Tombs' (*P*) signals death, and in 'To His Love' the last stanza packs into five lines the horrible death, the memories of flowery meadows in Gloucestershire and the need to forget the sight of the loved one's mangled body. The flowers become the effort to forget while at the same time they symbolise the memories that made the dead man precious. The speed of Gurney's lines leaves little time to construct metaphors; instead there are elisions, summaries, withdrawals into a private world, all tumbled together in images of pain. The strength of his verse lies in the depth of the emotion conveyed, flashes of reality rather than imagery conveyed in the terse lines.

Robert Graves and Siegfried Sassoon, the 'Two Fusiliers', were close friends once, with similar experiences at the Front. Graves's output is smaller, most of it left out of his later collections of verse. The tone is dry, the images spare, pared down (in 'Recalling War' (*C*) the war is 'an infection of the common sky') as if the poet wrote in some reluctance, wishing to leave the whole ghastly experience behind him.

By contrast Sassoon's output was considerable, driven as he was by his hatred of the war. A number of his poems are in fact grim anecdotes, usually with a pay-off line ('and die – in bed' – 'Base Details'; 'His face is trodden deeper in the mud' – 'Glory of Women'; 'Such men have lost all patriotic feeling' – 'Lamentations'; and of course 'But he did for them both by his plan of attack' – 'The General'). Yet the tense style still leaves room for telling images of death, in action usually, because that was Sassoon's first concern ('butchered, frantic gestures of the dead' – 'Counter Attack' (*C*); 'a trickling peace,/Gently and slowly washing life away' – 'The Death Bed' (which can be found in his *Collected Poems*, London, 1984)).

The metaphors are used not to soften the terrible impact of the image of death, but to strengthen it. Thus there is harmony between Sassoon's aim and his imagery – both have the same purpose, of driving home the truth about the war.

In Isaac Rosenberg's poetry there is no explicit message, as its first object is a description of the horrors of war. Because his aim is to describe, to convey the reality of what he saw, his poems are rich in images that arrest the reader's attention and remain in his memory ('Blind fingers loose an iron cloud' – deathly shells falling on the soldiers in 'Marching'; the extended metaphor of a wild dance in 'Louse Hunting' (*P*); the larksong 'showering' like a refreshing rain on the men's upturned faces in 'Returning, We Hear the Larks'; 'the swift iron burning bee' of the bullets draining the men's life blood in 'Dead Man's Dump'). This last great poem may of course be seen as a metaphor of the journey to death, taken here through a landscape filled with death.

Though much of Rosenberg's poetry is descriptive, inasmuch as he aims to convey the sights and sounds of war, its distinctive quality is due to the clarity of his intellect that rises beyond the reality of his vision.

In Wilfred Owen's poetry the function of the image is not just to describe, to evoke a picture – though he too wishes his readers to see the hell the soldiers inhabit. His main object, however, is not to turn us merely into spectators, but to force us to share, at least at second hand, the suffering of the men at the Front. The recurring images of dreams, of drowning ('As under a green sea' – 'Dulce Et Decorum Est'; 'My soul looked down from a great height' – 'The Show' (*P*); 'we have perished/Sleeping, and walk hell' – 'Mental Cases' (*C*)) stress the nightmare quality of such living. The equation of sleep with death finds its fullest expression in the great 'Strange Meeting'. Though in 'Asleep' (*C*) for a man shot as he lay asleep death might be seen as a desirable rest, yet there are disturbing images of blood and decay ('the slow, stray blood . . . like ants on track'; 'his thin and sodden head/Confuses . . . with the low mould') which will not permit the glib assumption of a happy release.

If a sleep, then a sleep with nightmares: the gibbering 'Mental Cases', the legless and armless boy in 'Disabled', the gassed man in 'Dulce Et Decorum Est', the blind, maimed man in 'A Terre' (*C*). This last poem ends with perhaps the clearest demand for pity stripped of all false sentimentality. The words have a grave, austere beauty: 'Carry my crying spirit till it's weaned/To do without what blood remained these wounds'. Such lines are hard to forget.

Charles Hamilton Sorley's few poems too have a harsh purity. He was concerned with death, but unlike Owen he rejected pity. His metaphors for death ('straight and steadfast signpost', 'a slate rubbed clean/A merciful putting away' – 'Two Sonnets' (*C*)) have a curiously brisk, matter-of-fact quality ('It is easy to be dead' – 'When you see the millions of the mouthless dead') almost a kind of jollity ('Strew your gladness on earth's bed,/So be merry, so be dead' – 'All the hills and vales along') echoed in the marching rhythm of this poem.

In Rupert Brooke's verse the rhetoric lies more in the emotions expressed than in the quality of the verse. If the sentiments are overblown, the imagery has a spare quality: the young men leaping into the cleansing war 'as swimmers into cleanness leaping' ('Peace'); death seen as 'A width, a shining peace' ('The Dead'). What richness there is lies in the heaping up of these pared down abstract images.

So many poets, so many poems, yet all preoccupied with one theme – the war and the death it brings. They all found their own individual voices, their own ways of dealing with the shattering events round them, and any comparisons, bringing out contrasts and seeking parallels, testify to the variety and richness of their verse, and to the unique qualities of every one of them.

Versification

Though the outbreak of the war produced a flood of 'war poems', most of these outpourings of patriotic verse adhered in form to the conventional rhyme and metre schemes of Georgian poetry. Rupert Brooke's accomplished sonnets are a model of that form.

We cannot say that as the war progressed such conventional forms were no longer acceptable. Some of the best, most moving poems of the war – Sorley's, Blunden's, Sassoon's lighter verse, a great deal of Owen's, as well as some of Thomas's, Gurney's and Rosenberg's – followed the traditional metrical and rhyme patterns. Moreover, there had been innovative poets well before the onset of the war.

There was Gerard Manley Hopkins (1844–89) whose imperfect rhymes and 'sprung rhythm', based on strong accentuation of a certain number of syllables per line, without any effort to regulate the intervening 'slack' syllables, were regarded by some as going against the natural rhythm of the English language. Hopkins's verse did not appear in print until 1918, yet his writing shows that there was a desire for a change in metrification before the turn of the century.

The work of the war poets, nonetheless, remains a worthwhile subject of study for its form as much as for its heart-breaking contents. These men paid close attention to the form of their poetry, as we can see from the drafts of some of the poems, for instance Owen's 'Dulce Et Decorum Est' and 'Strange Meeting'. The latter in particular cost the author a great deal of trouble. He seems to have been engaged on another poem parallel with this one, of which several versions have been preserved. (Details of this may be found in Owen's *Poems*, edited by Edmund Blunden, first published in 1931, and Jon Silkin in *The Penguin Book of First World War Poetry* prints the manuscript with corrections.)

It is clear that the form of his verse mattered to Owen greatly. The pararhymes and assonances were carefully chosen. Critics have advanced different reasons for their use, but whether their echoing sound helps to build in the readers' minds the image of the tunnel, or whether the sub-conscious feeling of dissatisfaction in the readers (by not hearing what they expected to hear – a perfect rhyme) gradually creates a mood of despair, the undoubted effect is considerable and not at all accidental. Surely the main point is that Owen conveyed his message ('My subject is War, and the pity of War') in a poem of very high quality, and that is why the message is read and remembered. The form is crucial to the contents.

For that reason perhaps, as the war went on, the nature of the poetry changed. Not only was free verse employed more often (by Sassoon, Rosenberg and Thomas in particular), but the imagery changed as well. Sorley's visions of death had been austere, unspecific; as the years passed and the poets felt called upon to bear witness to the horrors of the trenches, they no longer spared their readers. Surely the horrors described could not be shown in the incongruous form of rhyming stanzas. Rosenberg's 'Dead Man's Dump' would lose its impact if the poet's images did not come tumbling out, horror upon horror, like the piles of corpses.

The images were not 'poetic', nor could the form be. There is fitness in matching the form to the contents, and such fitness is to be found here.

Part 4

Hints for study

Reading the poets of the First World War

These Notes have for their subject not one poet, but a whole large group, and you will have to decide on your approach to their verse. If you are working on an essay, you are free to choose whether to concentrate on one poet or consider the group as a whole. If you are preparing for an examination, however, the choice is not entirely yours. You might consider concentrating on one or two of the major war poets (Owen and Sassoon, say). You should also be ready to deal with some aspects of the work of these poets as a group: perhaps the role played by nature in their verse, or the war as perceived by these soldier poets and as seen by the civilians.

Whatever the purpose of your study, your first step should be to make yourself familiar with as much of their work as you can manage within the time available to you. The volume of their verse is quite considerable, and the amount of reading expected of you may seem daunting.

The object of these Notes is to help you select, while making sure you include in your reading the poems that are essential to your understanding of these writers and that you will be expected to know well. As is mentioned in 'A note on the texts' (p. 14 above), the poems discussed in Part 2, 'Summaries', of these Notes can all be found in the six anthologies of First World War verse listed there. To be precise, all but eight of them are included in either I. M. Parsons's *Men who March Away* (*C*) or in Jon Silkin's *Penguin Book of First World War Poetry* (*P*). A great many of them are inevitably included in all the anthologies listed, and each collection also contains other poems well worth your attention.

That being the case, your best course is to get hold of the two anthologies mentioned above. Using these Notes as your guide, work your way through both of them, reading with special care the poems discussed in Part 2 of these Notes. They were chosen as representative of the individual poets, of the thoughts and emotions shared by many of them, and also as poems which a student might be expected to know.

Inevitably, as you leaf through the anthologies you will find yourself reading other poems as well, apart from those discussed here. This is all to the good; your reading should extend beyond the narrow confines of question-spotting, if you are to understand the nature of these poets' hold on their readers for so many decades.

One point should be made here, and stressed again and again. As you read, keep a note-pad by you and make a note of anything that arrests your attention (write down the author, the title, and the page number). Otherwise you will waste time later, searching for an elusive image or line.

Even at this early stage, perhaps while reading some of the poems for the first time, you may find yourself drawn to certain poets or to certain aspects of their poetry, and may thus decide quite early on what direction your study will take. You may find the list of sample examination questions (see below, p. 82) useful in helping you decide. Read it through as you carry on with your first reading of the poems. Even at this stage this exercise will help you identify the areas of interest to you.

While copying the lines that attract your attention, remember that you might wish to quote some of them to support your arguments later. As you may be answering questions while under pressure in an examination, make your quotations brief, easy to memorise. While examiners are assumed to favour the use of quotations (as proving the candidate's close knowledge of the text), they are certainly not fond of misattributions and inaccurate quotations. Better refer to a line indirectly by paraphrasing it rather than misquote.

As well as reading the poetry, you should also acquire some knowledge of the background of the First World War. Part 1, 'Introduction', of these Notes is a sketch of the course of the war, and most of the anthologies listed below in Part 5, 'Suggestions for further reading', include information on the background to the war. But to gain some idea of the reality of the trenches, essential to your understanding of the poetry, you cannot do better than read the first-hand accounts of the war by three of the poets discussed in these Notes. Robert Graves's *Goodbye to All That* and Edmund Blunden's *Undertones of War* are both autobiographical, while Siegfried Sassoon's *Memoirs of an Infantry Officer* is a fictionalised account of his experiences. All three are beautifully written, illuminating and informative.

Your preliminary reading done, go over your notes (which should contain your own reactions to the poems, as well as any quotations that struck you as relevant) and then read again the list of questions at the end of this section.

Consider now which poets appeal to you most, and which aspects of this remarkable poetry interest you. Make a note of your preferences, and try to rephrase them as essay titles or examination questions. You will find this exercise surprisingly helpful in giving shape to diffuse thoughts.

If you decide to concentrate on one or two individual poets, you will do well to read more of their work than just the poems discussed in the 'Summaries' above. The bibliographies in Part 5 below will help you, and you will find that most of the major poets have been reissued in paperback in recent years. By all means read any biography available, but remember that what really counts is the poetry and your thorough knowledge of it. To know the poems is to form your own opinions about them, and it is these that the examiners are interested in. No amount of regurgitated literary criticism can make up for your own fresh views, always supported by accurate references to the poems. Your essay, or examination answer, must show that you have read the poems for yourself, thought about them, and formulated your thoughts carefully into a coherent whole.

Answering the questions

Thinking about the questions at the start of an examination is as important as writing down the answers. Consider each question carefully, testing your knowledge and the strength of your reactions in your mind. *Never* decide to answer a question on the strength of a quotation you want to use. Instead, sketch out briefly your answer, stating the line of your argument first and then developing it paragraph by paragraph, constantly referring back to the question to make sure you are offering an answer to it. End by summing up your argument. (If you find yourself short of time at the end of the examination, most examiners will accept your sketch outline as part of your answer and judge it together with the incomplete answer.)

As timing is important in an examination, use at least the first fifteen minutes in deciding which questions to answer and formulating your answers in your mind. Then answer each question in turn, allocating to each roughly the same share of the time available, but leaving yourself sufficient time at the end to read through your answers and correct any spelling errors and rectify omissions.

Do not be afraid to disagree with a question; if you feel strongly enough about it and can show your reasons for disagreeing, go ahead, making sure you formulate your thoughts clearly, in a logical order. After all, the examiners want you to show that you know the poems and have thought about them. You must make sure, however, that you can put forward a coherent argument, and are not taking the line of opposition just to impress the examiners!

If you admire a poet's work, say so, and explain specifically which aspects of his work attract you. It is a common mistake (found all too often in the literary pages of the 'quality' Sunday papers) to assume that one has to demolish a work to prove one's own ability. It is far more difficult to praise intelligently than to savage a book by a piece of witticism. There-fore, never be afraid to show your enthusiasm, as long as you support it by thoughtful comments.

If you have any time to spare in the days before your examination, a practice run in answering examination questions is reassuring and helpful in developing the skill of formulating your answers. Your teacher may be able to let you see earlier examination papers and advise you on the time usually allowed for the examination. (You might also like to answer one or two of the questions in the list below: the more practice you have in this the better.)

Choose your question, decide on the length of time you will allow yourself for answering it, and settle down to work. Sketch out your argument briefly, check that it answers the question, and start writing, doing your best as you would in an examination. If you find yourself running out of time you will have to rethink your technique, tighten up your arguments and try to be more concise in your writing. Practice, as they say, makes perfect: it certainly makes the work easier and gives you confidence.

Specimen questions

(1) Compare and contrast the poetry of Wilfred Owen and Siegfried Sassoon as anti-war statements.

(2) Consider Blunden's '1916 seen from 1921' and Graves's 'Recalling War': what do these two poems tell you about their authors and about their war experiences?

(3) Consider the difference in the reactions to the war of the soldiers at the Front and the women in Britain in the light of two poems: Gurney's 'To His Love' and Mew's 'The Cenotaph'. You may refer to other poets if you wish.

(4) The Flanders poppy became a symbol of the war. Do you think this use is appropriate?

(5) Discuss in detail Wilfred Owen's 'Strange Meeting', paying special attention to his emendations.

(6) Do you see Edward Thomas's 'As the team's head brass' as a war poem?

(7) Can the poets of the First World War be considered as a group? Give your reasons for or against.

(8) Discuss the significance of Rupert Brooke's '1914' Sonnets as political statements and verse models on their publication and later.

(9) Julian Grenfell's 'Into Battle' and Charles Hamilton Sorley's 'All the hills and vales along' were both written during 1915; discuss the two poems, contrasting their form and message.

(10) Do you think women's poetry of the First World War has intrinsic merit?

(11) Discuss your favourite poem by one of these war poets, giving reasons for your preference.

Specimen answer

(2) Consider Blunden's '1916 seen from 1921' and Graves's 'Recalling War': what do these two poems tell you about their authors and their war experiences?

Even after just one reading we are struck by the difference between these two poems recalling the war. Blunden's '1916 seen from 1921' tells first of the poet's life back in England, two years after the end of the war. He is lonely, isolated from the people round him by the war horrors he remembers. His friends are all dead, the pleasures of his old life in England – his books, the countryside – have lost their power to delight him, and he is alone. The desolate landscape of the battlefield is still vivid to him, and he remembers in detail the broken shrines with their plaster figures of saints ('bright as blood'), the lizard on the hot path, the shrine of the Virgin where he and his best friend (presumably also killed in the war) used to find refuge from the war, sleeping in the warm sun.

Graves's poem was written some twenty years' later, by which time the memories of the war had grown more distant. The first stanza makes light of his war wounds ('Entrance and exit wounds are silvered clean': Graves had been severely wounded, shot clean through the lung, and nearly died) as well as of other men's injuries.

The war is now just a part of his memories of the past, part of the natural pattern of events seen more clearly at a distance (in one of the outstanding images of the poem he sees himself looking back and seeing the pattern of events emerge, like a traveller who had lost his way during the night, turning back in the morning and seeing his path clearly on the hillside).

Instead of Blunden's vivid memories of the ravaged landscape Graves remembers the effect of the war on young men like himself. The threat of death brought to them a freedom, indeed a licence to enjoy the pleasures of a life that might be cut short at any moment. Suddenly all such things – love, romance, good food and wine, bodily comforts – demanded to be enjoyed, and the young men strutted about, flaunting their valour and sexual power. All the old certainties of religion, of a fixed moral code had gone, the world had gone mad, and it seemed their duty to go mad as well. (We notice that all his descriptions are general: he always uses the pronoun 'we', not 'I'.)

The poems are very different, then: Blunden's a lament for the loss of happiness, of life itself, and Graves's a recollection of collective madness, remembered soberly and with detachment, without a trace of self-pity, but with a grim thought for the future, a warning given with the authority of past experience.

We cannot account for the difference by a disparity in their war experiences. Both of them had a remarkably long active service on the

Western Front, longer than most men's (because they survived). Blunden was awarded a Military Cross for bravery, Graves was severely wounded, indeed given up for dead – no safe jobs behind the lines for them.

We can only account for the difference by the two men's characters. Blunden was a gentle, introspective young man, probably young for his age (he was just a year younger than Graves), as witness the protective bearing of his fellow officers towards him, about which we read in his *Undertones of War*. Isolated by his war experiences from the people round him at home, he mourns his dead comrades and he mourns also the loss of own youth. Ironically, the recollection of the little shrine somewhere on the Western Front where he and his best friend used to hide and sleep when off-duty, brings a liveliness, almost a jollity to his sombre thoughts.

Graves, on the other hand, may have had 'a good war', enjoyed what was on offer (though his recollections in *Goodbye to All That* belie the strutting attitude of this poem. Reserved and fastidious, passionate about literature, he spent his home leaves reading, writing and climbing in Wales).

He looks back on the war with detachment, seeing an act of collective madness, a breakdown of values. Against this he sees the destruction caused by the war as the wilful action of a destructive child, nothing more. The wounds have healed, the dead are long dead, but the madness is remembered, and appropriately sombre forecasts are made for the future.

The basic difference, then, is between a man of feeling, emotional, vulnerable, and a reserved, disciplined man of thought whose reaction to the war is a considered weighing-up of its causes and the likelihood of its recurrence. In their different ways, appealing either to our sympathy or to our desire to understand, the two poems represent two equally valid reactions to the horrors of war.

Part 5

Suggestions for further reading

Anthologies

FULLER, SIMON (ED.): *The Poetry of War*, BBC/Longman, London, 1990.

GARDNER, BRIAN (ED.): *Up the Line to Death: the War Poets 1914–1918*, Methuen, London, 1976, re–issued 1986.

GLOVER, JON and SILKIN, JON (EDS): *The Penguin Book of First World War Prose*, Penguin Books, Harmondsworth, 1990.

HARRISON, MICHAEL and STUART–CLARK, CHRISTOPHER (EDS): *The New Dragon Book of Verse*, OUP, Oxford, 1977.

HEWETT, R. (ED.): *A Choice of Poets: an Anthology of Poets from Wordsworth to the Present Day*, Harrap, London, 1968, re–issued by Thomas Nelson & Sons, London, 1984 (Harrap's New Outlook Series).

MARTIN, CHRISTOPHER: *War Poems*, Collins Educational, London, 1991.

PARSONS, I. M. (ED.): *Men who March Away: Poems of the First World War*, Heinemann Educational Books, London, 1965, re–issued by Chatto, London, 1965, paperback 1993.

REILLY, CATHERINE W. (ED.): *Scars Upon My Heart: Women's Poetry and Verse of the First World War*, Virago, London, 1981.

SILKIN, JON (ED.): *The Penguin Book of First World War Poetry*, 2nd edition, Penguin Books, Harmondsworth, 1981.

STALLWORTHY, JON (COMP.): *The Oxford Book of War Poetry*, OUP, Oxford, 1984.

STEPHEN, MARTIN (ED.): *'Never Such Innocence': Poems of the First World War*, J. M. Dent, London, 1993 (Everyman Library).

Individual authors

BLUNDEN, EDMUND: *Selected Poems*, edited by Robyn Marsack, paperback, Carcanet, Manchester, 1982.

—: *Undertones of War*, Cobden–Sanderson, London, 1928, re–issued by Penguin Books, Harmondsworth, 1982 (Penguin Modern Classics).

BROOKE, RUPERT: *Collected Poems*, with a memoir by Edward Marsh, Sidgwick & Jackson, London, 1918. 4th revised edition with an introduction by Gavin Ewart, paperback, Macmillan, London, 1992 (Papermac).

—: *Poetical Works*, edited by Sir Geoffrey Keynes, paperback, Faber, London, 1970.

—: *Poetical Works*, new edition, Wordsworth Books, London, 1994 (Wordsworth Poetry Library).

—: *1914 and Other Poems*, paperback edition, Helion Books, Solihull, 1994.

GRAVES, ROBERT: *Collected Poems*, paperback edition, Cassell, London, 1992.

—: *Selected Poems*, edited by Patrick Quinn, Carcanet, Manchester, 1995.

—: *Selected Poems*, edited by Paul O'Prey, Penguin Books, Harmondsworth, 1992 (Penguin Modern Classics).

—: *Collected Writings on Poetry*, edited by Paul O'Prey, Carcanet, Manchester, 1995.

—: *Goodbye to All That*, new edition, Cassell, London, 1957; paperback edition, Penguin Books, Harmondsworth, 1990.

GURNEY, IVOR: *Collected Poems*, edited by P. J. Kavanagh, OUP, Oxford, 1982.

—: *Poems*, with a memoir by Edmund Blunden, Hutchinson, London, 1954.

—: *Selected Poems*, edited by P. J. Kavanagh, paperback, OUP, Oxford, 1990 (Oxford Poets).

—: *Severn and Somme: War's Embers*, Carcanet, Manchester, 1987.

—: *Letters*, edited by R. K. Thornton, Carcanet, Manchester, 1990.

OWEN, WILFRED: *Poems*, with a memoir by Edmund Blunden, Chatto, London, 1963.

—: *Poems*, edited by Jon Stallworthy, Hogarth Press, London, 1985; paperback edition, Chatto, London, 1990 (Chatto Poetry).

—: *Poetical Works*, paperback, Wordsworth Books, London, 1994 (Wordsworth Poetry Library).

—: *War Poems*, edited by Jon Stallworthy, paperback, Chatto, London, 1994.

—: *War Poems*, edited by Jon Silkin, Sinclair-Stevenson, London, 1994.

—: *Selected Poetry and Prose*, edited by Jennifer Breen, paperback, Routledge, London, 1988 (Routledge English Texts).

—: *Selected Poems*, Bloomsbury, London, 1995 (Bloomsbury Poetry Classics).

ROSENBERG, ISAAC: *Collected Works*, edited by Ian Parsons, Hogarth Press, London, 1984; paperback edition, Chatto, London, 1989.

SASSOON, SIEGFRIED: *Collected Poems, 1908–1956*, 2nd edition, Faber, London, 1961; paperback, 1984.

—: *War Poems*, arranged and introduced by Rupert Hart-Davis, Faber, London, 1983; paperback edition, 1984.

—: *Memoirs of a Fox-Hunting Man*, paperback edition, Faber, London 1977.

—: *Memoirs of an Infantry Officer*, paperback edition, Faber, London 1965.

—: *Complete Memoirs of George Sherston*, paperback edition, Faber, London, 1972.

SORLEY, CHARLES HAMILTON: *Collected Poems*, edited by Jean Moorcroft Wilson, Cecil Woolf, London, 1985.

—: *Poems and Selected Letters*, edited by Hilda D. Spear, paperback edition, Blackness Press, Dundee, 1978.

THOMAS, EDWARD: *Collected Poems*, edited by R. George Thomas, OUP, Oxford, 1978.

—: *Collected Poems*, edited with a foreword by Walter de la Mare, Faber, London, 1979, reset 1991.

—: *Poetical Works*, Wordsworth Books, London, 1994 (Wordsworth Poetry Library).

—: *Selected Poetry and Prose*, edited by David Wright, Penguin Books, Harmondsworth, 1981 (Penguin English Library).

—: *Language not to be Betrayed: selected prose*, edited by Edna Longley, Carcanet, Manchester, 1981.

Biography (including letters) and criticism

BLUNDEN, EDMUND: *War Poets, 1914–1918*, Longman for the British Council, London, 1958 (Writers and Their Work, No. 100).

GIDDINGS, ROBERT: *The War Poets*, Bloomsbury, London, 1988, paperback, 1990.

GURNEY, IVOR: *Letters*, edited by R. K. Thornton, Carcanet, Manchester, 1990.

HARRIS, PIPPA (ED.): *Song of Love; the letters of Rupert Brooke and Noel Olivier*, Bloomsbury, London, 1991.

LEHMANN, JOHN: *The English Poets of the First World War*, Thames & Hudson, London, 1981.

OWEN, WILFRED: *Selected Letters*, edited by John Ball, paperback, OUP, Oxford, 1986.

SEYMOUR-SMITH, (MARTIN): *Robert Graves: His Life and Work*, Bloomsbury, London, 1995.

STALLWORTHY, JON: *Wilfred Owen: A Biography*, paperback new edition, OUP, Oxford, 1988 (Oxford Paperbacks).

Background reading and viewing

Fiction:

BARBUSSE, HENRI: *Under Fire* (*Le Feu*, Paris, 1916), translated by Fitzwater Wray, Dent, London, 1917.

BRITTAIN, VERA: *Testament of Youth: an Autobiographical Story of the*

Years 1900–1925, Gollancz, London, 1933; paperback, Arrow Books, London, 1960.

HAŠEK, JAROSLAV: *The Good Soldier Švejk* (Osudy dobrého vojáka *Švejka*, Prague, 1921–23), translated by Paul Selver, Penguin Books, Harmondsworth, 1939.

REMARQUE, ERICH MARIA: *All Quiet on the Western Front* (*Im Westen nichts neues*, Berlin, 1929), translated by A. W. Wheen, Putnam, London, 1929; paperback edition, Pan Books, London, 1987 (Picador Classics).

Plays:

LITTLEWOOD, JOAN: *Oh What a Lovely War!* (staged 1963), Methuen, London, 1965.

SHERRIFF, R. C.: *Journey's End* (staged 1928), Gollancz, London, 1928; Penguin Books, Harmondsworth, 1983.

Films:

All Quiet on the Western Front (1930), directed by Lewis Milestone.

La Grande Illusion (1937), directed by Jean Renoir.

The author of these notes

HANA SAMBROOK was educated at the Charles University in Prague and the University of Edinburgh. She worked as an editor in educational publishing and was for some years on the staff of Edinburgh University Library. Now a freelance editor in London, she is the author of several York Notes, including Sylvia Plath's *Selected Works*.